PREVENTION MAGAZINE'S

QUICK & HEALTHY LOW-FAT COOKING

Easy One-Dish Meals

*Time-saving, nourishing one-pot dinners from
the stovetop, oven and salad bowl*

❧ ❧ ❧

Rodale Press, Inc.
Emmaus, Pennsylvania

QUICK AND HEALTHY LOW-FAT COOKING

Managing Editor: JEAN ROGERS

Vice President and Editorial Director: DEBORA T. YOST

Art Director: JANE COLBY KNUTILA

Associate Art Directors: FAITH HAGUE, ELIZABETH OTWELL

Easy One-Dish Meals was produced by Rebus, Inc.

Recipe Development: CAROL PRAGER, AMANDA CUSHMAN

Editor: MARYA DALRYMPLE

Writer: BONNIE J. SLOTNICK

Art Director and Designer: JUDITH HENRY

Production Editors: SUE PAIGE, MICHELE HEARNS

Photographer: ANGELO CAGGIANO

Food Stylists: WILLIAM L. SMITH, A. J. BATTIFARANO, HELEN JONES,
    DIANE SIMONE VEZZA

Prop Stylist: FRANCINE MATALON-DEGNI

Nutritional Analyses: HILL NUTRITION ASSOCIATES

Library of Congress Cataloging-in-Publication Data

Easy one-dish meals: time-saving, nourishing one-pot dinners from the
stovetop, oven and salad bowl / edited by Jean Rogers.
    p.   cm. — (Prevention magazine's quick & healthy low-fat cooking)
Includes index.
ISBN 0–87596–324–2 hardcover
ISBN 0–87596–325–0 paperback
1. Casserole cookery.   2. Low-fat diet—Recipes.   3. Quick and easy
cookery. I. Rogers, Jean [date]. II. Prevention (Emmaus, Pa.) III. Series:
Prevention magazine's quick & healthy low-fat cooking
(Series)
TX693.E18   1996
641.8'21—dc20   95–49515

Distributed in the book trade by St. Martin's Press

2   4   6   8   10   9   7   5   3   1   hardcover
2   4   6   8   10   9   7   5   3   1   paperback

CONTENTS

❧ ❧ ❧

Hearty Soups & Stews 18

All-in-a-bowl meals—gumbo, chowder,
chili and more

Satisfying Oven Dinners 44

Casseroles, pastas and pot pie—old favorites
and new delights from the oven

Stir-Fries & Other Skillet Meals 70

Popular pan dinners inspired by the world's
great cuisines

Main-Course Salads 100

Solid, substantial meals featuring pasta and grains,
chicken and beef, greens and fruit

PREFACE

❧ ❧ ❧

Does the end of a hectic workday find you facing this scenario: You rush home and rummage through the fridge for a meal you can put together quickly without a lot of stress. There's not much to choose from, so you end up throwing a package of ready-made food into the microwave—for the third time this week. Sure, it was easy, but you're not really satisfied. And neither is your family.

The ideal solution would be to get a healthy home-cooked meal on the table with just as little effort. *Easy One-Dish Meals* lets you do just that. In fact, one-dish meals are tailor-made for cooks like you. They let you serve balanced, tasty dinners without spending countless hours planning, preparing and cleaning up. In short, one-dish meals are perfect for today's busy lifestyle. They even make entertaining a breeze. Everyone can relax and enjoy, including the cook.

The recipes in this book update a classic way to cook and address our modern health and dietary concerns. This is the way families used to cook, but now it's faster, easier and healthier. With one-pot cooking, taste is enhanced, never sacrificed. Dishes are lower in cholesterol and fat but still deliver full flavor satisfaction.

Easy One-Dish Meals preserves our interest in regional and traditional American fare, but also reflects our desire to experience different ethnic cuisines. It is not uncommon for today's cook to literally use ingredients from all over the globe. Fortunately, these ingredients are readily available in most major supermarkets. And that's the terrific thing about these recipes—no special shopping is needed to make any dish.

Using this book, you can feast on old favorites and discover new or exotic dishes. This is food you can be proud to serve to anyone who shares your table.

Jean Rogers

JEAN ROGERS
Food Editor
Prevention Magazine Health Books

INTRODUCTION

એઠ એઠ એઠ

It is always a pleasure to put a delicious, well-balanced (and well-appreciated) dinner on the table, but your delight can quickly turn to dismay if you find yourself in the kitchen afterward faced with a sinkful of plates, bowls, pots, pans and miscellaneous utensils. And even if you love to cook, the task of choosing salads and vegetables to complement your everyday main dishes can lose its charm after years of dutiful meal planning. The ingenious solution to both situations is an all-in-one dinner from the stovetop, oven or salad bowl. The recipes you'll find in this volume offer something for every season and every occasion—and they're tempting combinations that go well beyond the usual franks and beans, hamburger casseroles and tuna-noodle concoctions sauced with canned cream-of-mushroom soup.

Such simple one-dish meals have been touted, at various times, as fuel-savers, time-savers and human-energy savers—and they do, indeed, conserve all three of these resources. But the challenge of combining the major components of a meal into one dish also sparks culinary creativity, resulting in such deliciously innovative recipes as the ones you'll find on these pages: a curry made with butternut squash (page 32), for example; a pot pie topped with crisp, delicate sheets of phyllo pastry (page 58); a toss of fresh tuna, pasta and feta cheese (page 80); and a salad made with lentils and lamb steak (page 102). Each recipe produces a well-rounded meal, and although you may wish to add some finishing touches, such as a good loaf of bread and a light dessert, you really don't have to do much more than set the table and sit down.

The recipes that follow fall into four categories: The soups, stews and chowders, found in the first chapter, are classic one-pot meals that feature meaty and meatless dishes, Italian and Mexican recipes and some regional American specialties. (With

the addition of pasta, rice or starchy vegetables, each of these bountiful bowls becomes a complete meal.) And the oven dinners in the second chapter are hardly common casseroles. They include roasted cod with cumin, ginger and cilantro; turkey, vegetables and pasta baked in paper packets; and an updated shepherd's pie with a Cheddar-gilded potato crust. In Chapter 3, you'll find skillet meals and a wholly different set of one-pot options: There are several Asian stir-fries; a vegetable-laden frittata (Italian-style omelet); a shrimp sauté; and a much-simplified version of cassoulet (the elaborate French baked bean dish). And while hearty eaters may tremble at the thought of dining on salad, the recipes in the fourth chapter are hardly lightweights: Choose from such satisfying combinations as salmon tossed with sesame noodles; Mexican Cobb salad with tuna; sliced sirloin with vegetables in a spicy Thai dressing; or a tasty sweet-and-white-potato salad with chunks of broiled chicken.

At first glance, it may appear that both the ingredient lists and the preparation times required for these recipes are somewhat longer than you may have expected. Don't forget, though, that you'll be turning out a full meal from a single recipe, and that you won't need to plan, shop for and cook separate side dishes. Be sure to notice that the cooking times for some traditionally time-consuming recipes—such as lamb stew and lasagna—have been trimmed considerably.

And for those especially pressed for time, the first section of the book (the next eight pages) offers six "crowd pleasing" one-dish recipes that can be made in advance. These special one-dish dinners are for six to eight people (the other recipes in the book each make four servings), and all freeze well. They are followed by information on the basic equipment needed for cooking and serving delicious one-dish meals.

Crowd Pleasers

There's a great sense of security in knowing you have a hearty meal for six or eight tucked away in the freezer. It gives you the freedom to take a few nights off from cooking, even to plan a casual gathering without ordering in the predictable pizza or Chinese food. Here are six simple one-dish recipes; each serves a small crowd and freezes well for up to a month.

MEXICAN BEEF STEW

❧ ❧ ❧

Even if you don't want to make this stew in advance and freeze it, you can still get a head start: The day before you intend to serve the stew, follow the recipe through Step 3. The next day, cook the rice (Step 4) while you reheat the stew, then complete Steps 5 and 6 of the recipe and ladle the stew over the freshly cooked rice.

- 3 teaspoons olive oil
- 2 pounds lean, well-trimmed beef chuck blade, cut into ½-inch cubes
- 1 teaspoon salt
- ¼ teaspoon freshly ground black pepper
- 2 medium onions, coarsely chopped
- 1 red bell pepper, coarsely chopped
- 2 medium zucchini, halved lengthwise and cut into ½-inch-thick slices
- 2 garlic cloves, minced
- 1 can (28 ounces) crushed tomatoes with juice
- 5 cups water
- 1½ tablespoons chili powder
- 1 tablespoon ground cumin
- 2 cups long-grain white rice
- 2 packages (10 ounces each) frozen corn kernels, thawed
- 2 tablespoons cornstarch dissolved in 2 tablespoons cold water
- ¼ cup fresh cilantro, chopped

1 In a Dutch oven or large, heavy saucepan, warm the oil over medium-high heat. Add the beef and sauté for 3 minutes, or until browned on all sides. Stir in ½ teaspoon of the salt and the black pepper.

2 Add the onions, bell peppers, zucchini and garlic, and cook for 5 minutes, or until the vegetables are softened.

3 Add the tomatoes and their juice, 1 cup of the water, the chili powder and cumin. Cover and bring to a boil; boil for 2 minutes. Reduce the heat to medium, partially cover and cook for 25 minutes, or until the beef is tender.

4 Meanwhile, in a medium saucepan, combine the rice with the remaining 4 cups water and the remaining ½ teaspoon salt; bring to a boil over medium heat. Cover the pan, reduce the heat to low and cook for 17 to 20 minutes, or until the rice is tender and the liquid absorbed.

5 When the beef is tender, add the corn to the stew and cook for 1 to 2 minutes, or until heated through.

6 Stir the cornstarch mixture to recombine it and add to the stew. Bring to a boil and cook, stirring, for 3 minutes, or until thickened.

7 Ladle the stew over the rice and sprinkle with the cilantro.

Per serving 476 calories, 11.7 g. fat, 3.6 g. saturated fat, 74 mg. cholesterol, 547 mg. sodium **Serves 8**

PASTA AND
WHITE BEAN STEW

❧ ❧ ❧

Orzo pasta, used in this savory stew, is roughly the size and shape of long-grain rice. You could also use *conchiglietti* (tiny shells) or *stelline* (tiny stars).

  2 teaspoons olive oil

  5 medium carrots, diced

  2 medium onions, chopped

  4 celery stalks, sliced

  3 garlic cloves, minced

  5 cups water

  2 cups defatted reduced-sodium chicken broth

  3 teaspoons fresh rosemary, chopped

  1 pound orzo or other small pasta

  2 cans (19 ounces each) white beans, rinsed and drained

1½ pounds kale, stemmed and chopped

  3 medium tomatoes, chopped

½ teaspoon salt

½ teaspoon freshly ground black pepper

¼ cup plus 2 tablespoons grated Parmesan cheese

1 In a Dutch oven or large, heavy saucepan, warm the oil over medium heat. Add the carrots, onions, celery and garlic, and cook for 3 minutes, or until the onions are softened.

2 Add the water, 1 cup of the broth and the rosemary. Increase the heat to medium-high and simmer for 2 minutes to blend the flavors.

3 Reduce the heat to medium, add the pasta and cook, stirring often, for 8 minutes, or according to package directions until al dente.

4 Add the beans, kale, tomatoes, salt, black pepper and remaining 1 cup broth. Cover and cook for 5 minutes longer, or until the kale is wilted. Serve with the Parmesan sprinkled on top.

Per serving 393 calories, 4.4 g. fat, 1.1 g. saturated fat, 3 mg. cholesterol, 650 mg. sodium **Serves 8**

CHICKEN FRICASSEE WITH RICOTTA-HERB DUMPLINGS

❧ ❧ ❧

For well-shaped, evenly sized dumplings, scoop up the dough with a ¼-cup dry measure (the kind you'd use for flour or sugar).

2 cups water

1 cup defatted reduced-sodium chicken broth

2 pounds skinless, boneless chicken breast halves, cut into 1-inch cubes

4 medium carrots, thinly sliced

2 celery stalks, thinly sliced

1 pound green beans, trimmed and halved

3 scallions, thinly sliced

2 tablespoons cornstarch

1 cup 1% low-fat milk

2 tablespoons chopped fresh dill

¾ teaspoon salt

¼ teaspoon freshly ground black pepper

2 teaspoons chopped fresh thyme or ¼ teaspoon dried thyme

1 package (10 ounces) frozen peas, thawed

1½ cups part-skim ricotta cheese

¾ cup all-purpose flour

3 tablespoons chopped Italian parsley

1 tablespoon melted butter or margarine

1 teaspoon baking powder

Fresh dill sprigs, for garnish (optional)

1 In a Dutch oven or a large, heavy saucepan, combine 1 cup of the water and the broth, and bring to a simmer over medium-high heat. Add the chicken and poach for 4 minutes, or until firm to the touch. Using a slotted spoon, transfer the chicken to a plate and set aside.

2 Add the carrots and celery to the pan, and cook for 3 minutes. Add the remaining 1 cup water, the green beans and scallions, and cook for 3 minutes longer, or until the vegetables are tender. Using a slotted spoon, transfer the vegetables to another plate.

3 In a small bowl, whisk together the cornstarch and milk, then whisk the cornstarch mixture into the hot broth. Add the dill, ½ teaspoon of the salt, the black pepper and thyme, and cook, stirring frequently, for 5 minutes, or until thickened.

4 Return the chicken and vegetables to the pan. Add the peas and stir to combine. Reduce the heat to medium, cover and cook for 5 minutes, or until the stew is hot.

5 While the chicken and vegetables are heating, make the dumpling dough. In a medium bowl, combine the ricotta, flour, parsley, butter or margarine, baking powder and remaining ¼ teaspoon salt; mix well with a fork. Drop the dough by ¼-cup portions onto the stew to make 16 dumplings. Cover the pan and cook over medium-low heat for 15 minutes, or until the dumplings are done to your taste (they will be moist). Garnish with fresh dill sprigs, if desired.

Per serving 330 calories, 7.2 g. fat, 3.8 g. saturated fat, 85 mg. cholesterol, 565 mg. sodium **Serves 8**

SAVE THAT DISH

You don't need to sacrifice your favorite baking dish to the freezer when you prepare one of these meals in advance: You can make a freezable, recyclable foil container instead, thus leaving the dish available for other uses. *Note:* Acidic foods, such as tomato sauces, may occasionally cause aluminum foil to discolor or pit.

For foods to be cooked in a baking dish, line the dish with heavy-duty foil, leaving enough overhang to enclose the food after cooking. When the food is cooked and cooled, bring the ends of the foil over the top and seal them together, then place the dish in the freezer. When the food is frozen solid, slip the foil-wrapped package out of the dish and seal it in a large plastic freezer bag. To reheat, remove the package from the bag and slip the foil-wrapped food back into the baking dish.

For a soup or stew, such as the chicken fricassee included here, follow the same procedure, ladling the cooked food into a foil-lined dish for freezing. You can reheat soups and stews in the oven, as above, or transfer them to a heavy saucepan, Dutch oven or skillet for reheating on the stove over medium heat. Stir frequently.

LASAGNA BOLOGNESE WITH TWO-TOMATO SAUCE

❧ ❧ ❧

This dish comes from the city of Bologna, nick-named *Bologna la grassa*—"Bologna the fat"—because of its inhabitants' lavish use of the local agricultural bounty, including cheeses, meats, milk, butter and eggs. Happily, some favorite Bolognese dishes can be easily adapted to today's health-conscious tastes. This lasagna could well come from "Bologna the lean but delicious."

2¼ ounces sun-dried tomatoes (not oil-packed)
1 pound lean ground beef
3 medium carrots, diced
1 medium onion, chopped
½ pound fresh mushrooms, sliced
2 celery stalks, diced
1 teaspoon fresh rosemary, chopped
1 teaspoon fresh thyme, chopped
½ teaspoon salt
¼ teaspoon freshly ground black pepper
1 can (16 ounces) crushed tomatoes with juice
½ cup water
1 bay leaf, preferably imported
1 cup 1% low-fat milk
½ cup defatted reduced-sodium chicken broth
2 tablespoons cornstarch dissolved in ¼ cup water
6 ounces no-cook lasagna noodles
2 ounces part-skim mozzarella cheese, shredded

1 Preheat the oven to 375°. In a small bowl, combine the sun-dried tomatoes with boiling water to cover and soak for 5 minutes to soften. When softened, drain and chop coarsely. Set aside.

2 Meanwhile, in a large no-stick skillet, combine the beef, carrots, onions, mushrooms, celery, rosemary, thyme, ¼ teaspoon of the salt and ⅛ teaspoon of the black pepper. Cook over medium-high heat, breaking up the meat with a spoon, for about 5 minutes, or until the beef is browned.

3 Add the crushed tomatoes and their juice, the chopped sun-dried tomatoes, the water and bay leaf. Reduce the heat to medium and cook, stirring occasionally, for 2 minutes to blend the flavors. Transfer the sauce to a large bowl.

4 Pour the milk, broth and cornstarch mixture into the large skillet and cook over medium heat, stirring,

for 2 minutes, or until the sauce thickens. Add the remaining ¼ teaspoon salt and ⅛ teaspoon black pepper; remove the skillet from the heat.

5 Spoon one-fourth of the meat sauce into an 11 x 7-inch baking dish. Place one-third of the noodles over the meat sauce, then pour one-third of the white sauce over the noodles. Repeat with two more layers of noodles and sauces, ending with the meat sauce.

6 Sprinkle the mozzarella on top and bake for 15 to 20 minutes, or until the cheese is bubbly.

Per serving 376 calories, 10.8 g. fat, 4.4 g. saturated fat, 54 mg. cholesterol, 521 mg. sodium **Serves 6**

Chicken-Vegetable Stroganoff

❧ ❧ ❧

For this light stroganoff, the sauce gets just a touch of sour cream; cornstarch serves as the real thickener.

2 teaspoons olive oil

2 pounds skinless, boneless chicken breast halves, cut into ½-inch cubes

3 leeks, split lengthwise, washed and thinly sliced

3 garlic cloves, minced

1 tablespoon plus 1 teaspoon fresh thyme, chopped

2 pounds all-purpose potatoes, peeled and cut into 1-inch pieces

1½ pounds shiitake mushrooms, thinly sliced

2 cups defatted reduced-sodium chicken broth

¾ teaspoon salt

½ teaspoon freshly ground black pepper

1 package (10 ounces) frozen peas, thawed

2 tablespoons cornstarch dissolved in ¼ cup cold water

3 tablespoons reduced-fat sour cream

1 tablespoon minced chives

1 In a Dutch oven or large, heavy saucepan, warm the oil over medium-high heat. Add the chicken and sauté for about 3 minutes, or until the chicken is lightly browned.

2 Add the leeks, garlic and thyme, and cook for 1 minute, or until the leeks are golden. Add the potatoes, mushrooms, broth, salt and black pepper; cover and bring to a boil. Boil for 2 minutes, then reduce the heat to medium-low and cook for 15 minutes longer, or until the potatoes are tender.

3 Add the peas and cornstarch mixture, and simmer, stirring, for 2 minutes.

4 Remove the pan from the heat and stir in the sour cream. Sprinkle with the chives before serving.

Per serving 300 calories, 4 g. fat, 1 g. saturated fat, 68 mg. cholesterol, 501 mg. sodium **Serves 8**

HEARTY VEGETARIAN CHILI

❧ ❧ ❧

Don't be put off by the long ingredient list: About one-third of it is dry ingredients—cocoa powder, chili powder and so on—which you can measure out and combine in advance. The cocoa powder echoes the use of chocolate in a Mexican *mole* sauce; feel free to alter the other seasonings—especially the hot ones— to taste. The yogurt, Cheddar, scallions and cilantro are optional additions to offer at the table.

- 2 teaspoons olive oil
- 4 medium carrots, thinly sliced
- 2 medium onions, chopped
- 1 pound fresh mushrooms, sliced
- 1 red bell pepper, cut into ½-inch dice
- 1 yellow bell pepper, cut into ½-inch dice
- 5 celery stalks, diced
- 2 garlic cloves, minced
- ¾ pound green cabbage, thinly sliced
- 1 tablespoon chili powder
- 1 tablespoon unsweetened cocoa powder
- 2 teaspoons ground cumin
- 1 teaspoon dried oregano
- ½ teaspoon ground cinnamon
- ⅛ teaspoon ground red pepper
- 2 cups quick-cooking pearl barley
- 2 cups defatted reduced-sodium chicken broth
- 1 can (28 ounces) plum tomatoes with juice
- 1 can (15¼ ounces) kidney beans, rinsed and drained
- 1 package (10 ounces) frozen corn kernels, thawed
- 1 package (10 ounces) frozen lima beans, thawed
- ½ teaspoon salt
- ¼ teaspoon freshly ground black pepper
- ½ cup plain low-fat yogurt (optional)
- 3 ounces Cheddar cheese, grated (optional)
- 3 scallions, thinly sliced (optional)
- ¼ cup chopped fresh cilantro (optional)

1 In a Dutch oven or large, heavy saucepan, warm the oil over medium-high heat. Add the carrots, onions, mushrooms, red and yellow bell peppers, celery and garlic, and stir to combine. Cover and cook for 7 minutes, or until the vegetables begin to soften.

2 Add the cabbage and cook for 2 minutes, or until the cabbage is wilted. Add the chili powder, cocoa powder, cumin, oregano, cinnamon and ground red pepper, and cook, stirring, for 2 minutes longer.

3 Reduce the heat to medium, add the barley, broth and tomatoes and their juice, and cook for 5 minutes, breaking up the tomatoes with a spoon.

4 Stir in the kidney beans, corn, lima beans, salt and black pepper. Reduce the heat to medium-low, cover and simmer for 10 minutes, or until the barley is tender.

5 Serve the chili with the yogurt, Cheddar cheese, scallions and cilantro for toppings, if desired.

Per serving 343 calories, 3.2 g. fat, 0.4 g. saturated fat, 0 mg. cholesterol, 605 mg. sodium **Serves 8**

EQUIPMENT FOR ONE-DISH MEALS

SOUPS AND STEWS

A large, heavy-gauge saucepan or a Dutch oven is ideal for making soups and stews. The pot shown here is enameled cast iron, an extremely durable material; a handsome pot like this one can go right from stovetop to table. If your pots are not quite so attractive, transfer the soup or stew to a tureen for serving. You'll also need a couple of ladles and spoons (some slotted) for mixing, skimming and serving.

OVEN DINNERS

Baking dishes should be sturdy—flameproof as well as heatproof, so they can go under the broiler—and easy to clean, too. The dishes shown here are all glass or ceramic, which retain heat well. The square baking dish, just right for four servings, comes to the table in its own wire-and-raffia "cradle." The shallow oval bakers are perfect for individual seafood gratins; the gold-colored miniature soufflé dish is available in larger sizes. On the right are traditional onion-soup crocks, which can also be used for baking single portions of macaroni and cheese.

SKILLET MEALS

Although a 10- or 12-inch no-stick skillet works just fine for many of the top-of-the-stove recipes in this book, a wok is a versatile addition to any kitchen. And it's not just useful for Asian stir-fries: A wok with a cover also makes an excellent steamer. The traditional wok ladle and spatula, as well as the oversized chopsticks, shown here, are handy accessories. For jobs such as toasting almonds or sesame seeds, or for reheating single portions, a smaller skillet is your best bet. A small, heavy pan like this one can also serve as a mallet for pounding meat or poultry cutlets.

MAIN-COURSE SALADS

This generously sized bowl lets you toss a salad without scattering it all over the table; made of glass, it shows off colorful ingredients without retaining odors (which can be a problem with a wooden bowl). Try some of the gadgets shown here to speed the job of preparing salad ingredients: The Italian *mezzaluna* (half-moon) chopper with its hollowed board is excellent for mincing fresh herbs; the white rotary mincer is useful for chopping herbs, onions or nuts on a cutting board; the peeler's swivel blade cuts closely with minimal pressure and has a device at one side for removing the eyes from potatoes.

Hearty Soups & Stews

❧ ❧ ❧

ALL-IN-A-BOWL MEALS—

GUMBO, CHOWDER, CHILI AND MORE

MILANESE PORK STEW WITH GREMOLATA

Pork Stew

2 cups water

1 cup long-grain white rice

Pinch of dried saffron

12 ounces lean, boneless pork loin, cut into ¾-inch cubes

½ teaspoon salt

¼ teaspoon freshly ground black pepper

1 tablespoon plus 1 teaspoon olive oil

1 medium onion, chopped

2 medium carrots, chopped

2 celery stalks, chopped

2 garlic cloves, minced

½ teaspoon dried basil

½ teaspoon dried thyme

1 bay leaf, preferably imported

½ cup white wine

1 strip (3 inches long) lemon zest

1 can (16 ounces) whole tomatoes in purée

½ cup defatted reduced-sodium chicken broth

8 ounces small white mushrooms, quartered

1 cup frozen peas

Gremolata

¼ cup chopped Italian parsley

1 tablespoon zest shaved with a vegetable peeler and cut into thin strips or 1 tablespoon grated zest

2 small garlic cloves, minced

Preceding pages: Basil Minestrone (recipe on page 28).

An Italian creation, *gremolata* is a delicious, fresh seasoning mixture made from citrus zest, garlic and parsley. It's most commonly used on osso buco (braised veal shanks) but is an equally fine complement to this rich-tasting pork stew.

1 In a medium saucepan, bring the water to a boil over high heat. Stir in the rice and saffron, and reduce the heat to medium-low; cover and simmer for 20 minutes, or until the rice is tender and the liquid is absorbed. Remove the rice from the heat and set aside, covered.

2 While the rice cooks, in a medium bowl, toss the pork with ¼ teaspoon of the salt and the black pepper. In a large, heavy saucepan, warm 2 teaspoons of the oil over medium-high heat until very hot but not smoking. Add the pork and sauté for 2 minutes, or until browned. With a slotted spoon, transfer the pork to a plate.

3 Add the remaining 2 teaspoons oil to the saucepan and warm over medium heat. Stir in the onions, carrots and celery; cover and cook, stirring occasionally, for 5 minutes, or until the vegetables begin to soften. Stir in the garlic, basil, thyme and bay leaf, and cook for 30 seconds. Add the wine and strip of lemon zest, and cook for 2 minutes, scraping up any browned bits from the bottom of the pan.

4 Add the tomatoes, broth and remaining ¼ teaspoon salt. Reduce the heat to medium-low and simmer, covered, for 20 minutes.

5 Stir in the mushrooms and simmer, uncovered, for 5 minutes. Stir in the peas and simmer for 5 minutes, or until the pork is cooked through.

6 Meanwhile, prepare the gremolata. In a small bowl, combine the parsley, lemon zest and garlic.

7 Divide the rice among 4 bowls or plates and top with the stew. Sprinkle some gremolata over each portion.

Preparation time 35 minutes • **Total time** 1 hour • **Per serving** 449 calories, 10.1 g. fat (20% of calories), 2.4 g. saturated fat, 50 mg. cholesterol, 658 mg. sodium, 4.9 g. dietary fiber, 131 mg. calcium, 5 mg. iron, 41 mg. vitamin C, 6.8 mg. beta-carotene • **Serves 4**

ASIAN CHICKEN NOODLE SOUP

1 tablespoon plus 1 teaspoon vegetable oil

12 ounces skinless, boneless chicken breast halves, thinly sliced

4 scallions, thinly sliced on the diagonal

2 garlic cloves, minced

1 teaspoon grated fresh ginger

2 cups thinly sliced small white mushrooms

3 cups defatted reduced-sodium chicken broth

2½ cups water

½ cup canned sliced bamboo shoots, rinsed and drained

¼ teaspoon crushed red pepper flakes

4 ounces fresh cappellini pasta

4 cups packed fresh spinach leaves, coarsely chopped

1 tablespoon balsamic vinegar

2 tablespoons reduced-sodium soy sauce

2 large egg whites, lightly beaten

½ teaspoon dark sesame oil

1 medium carrot, shredded

¼ cup chopped fresh cilantro

This bountiful soup is made with cappellini (angel-hair pasta) instead of Asian noodles. If you can get Chinese or Japanese noodles (shown below), try them in this soup; cook the noodles according to the package directions.

1 In a large saucepan, warm the vegetable oil over medium-high heat until very hot but not smoking. Add the chicken and stir-fry for 2 minutes, or until opaque. Add the scallions, garlic and ginger, and stir-fry for 30 seconds, or until fragrant. Add the mushrooms and stir-fry for 1 minute, or until tender.

2 Add the broth, water, bamboo shoots and red pepper flakes, and bring to a boil over high heat. Stir in the pasta and spinach, and cook for 1 minute, or until the pasta is tender and the spinach is just wilted. Reduce the heat to medium and stir in the vinegar and soy sauce. Stir in the beaten egg whites and simmer, stirring, for 1 minute. Stir in the sesame oil.

3 Ladle the soup into 4 bowls and top with the carrots and cilantro.

Preparation time 20 minutes • **Total time** 35 minutes • **Per serving** 293 calories, 7.3 g. fat (23% of calories), 1.1 g. saturated fat, 70 mg. cholesterol, 952 mg. sodium, 4.2 g. dietary fiber, 122 mg. calcium, 5 mg. iron, 31 mg. vitamin C, 6.5 mg. beta-carotene • **Serves 4**

Japanese dried noodles: *tomoshiraga somen* (fine wheat noodles), *soba* (buckwheat noodles) and *udon* (wheat noodles).

Two types of quick-cooking Chinese dried egg noodles, or *dan mian*. Those on the right are made with wheat flour.

GULF COAST SEAFOOD GUMBO WITH RICE

2¾ cups water

1 cup long-grain white rice

1 tablespoon plus 1 teaspoon olive oil

2 ounces trimmed Canadian bacon, diced

2 tablespoons all-purpose flour

1 medium onion, chopped

1 medium green bell pepper, diced

1 medium red bell pepper, diced

1 celery stalk, diced

3 garlic cloves, minced

½ teaspoon dried thyme or 1 teaspoon fresh thyme

½ teaspoon freshly ground black pepper

¼ teaspoon salt

1 cup defatted reduced-sodium chicken broth

1 cup sliced frozen okra

1 cup drained canned whole tomatoes, coarsely chopped, with juice reserved

1 bay leaf, preferably imported

½ teaspoon hot-pepper sauce

8 ounces skinned red snapper fillet, cut into 1½-inch pieces

8 ounces medium shrimp, peeled and deveined, with tails attached

2 scallions, chopped

Fresh thyme sprigs, for garnish (optional)

Gumbo, like so many of Lousiana's beloved dishes, combines French and African ingredients and methods with the bounty of local produce, seafood and meats. It is based on a browned flour mixture called a *roux* and contains crisp sliced okra, a vegetable that was brought to America by African slaves. Tomatoes, bell peppers, onions and celery go into most gumbos; in addition to the fish and shrimp used here, some Louisiana cooks incorporate crabmeat, oysters, ham or sausage, chicken or duck.

1 In a medium saucepan, bring 2 cups of the water to a boil over high heat. Stir in the rice and reduce the heat to medium-low; cover and simmer for 20 minutes, or until all the liquid is absorbed. Remove the pan from the heat; set aside, covered, until the gumbo is ready.

2 While the rice is cooking, in a large, heavy saucepan, warm the oil over medium heat. Add the bacon and cook for 2 minutes, or until golden and crisp. With a slotted spoon, transfer the bacon to a small bowl and set aside.

3 Reduce the heat to medium-low and stir the flour into the pan. Cook, stirring frequently, for 3 to 4 minutes, or until the flour mixture turns a deep golden brown. (Be careful not to scorch the flour.)

4 Stir in the onions, bell peppers, celery, garlic, thyme, black pepper and salt. Cover and cook, stirring occasionally, for 5 minutes.

5 Stir in the remaining ¾ cup water, the broth, okra, tomatoes and their juice, bay leaf and hot-pepper sauce. Return to a simmer, cover and cook for 10 minutes, or until the mixture thickens and the vegetables are tender. Stir in the snapper and shrimp, and cook for 5 minutes, or until the seafood is opaque. Return the bacon to the pan.

6 Divide the rice among 4 bowls. Serve the gumbo over the rice, and sprinkle with the scallions. Garnish with fresh thyme sprigs, if desired.

Preparation time 25 minutes • **Total time** 40 minutes • **Per serving** 418 calories, 7.8 g. fat (17% of calories), 1.4 g. saturated fat, 98 mg. cholesterol, 731 mg. sodium, 4.4 g. dietary fiber, 147 mg. calcium, 5 mg. iron, 76 mg. vitamin C, 1.1 mg. beta-carotene • **Serves 4**

CHICKEN PRIMAVERA STEW

1 small chicken (2½ to 3 pounds), skinned and cut into 8 pieces

2½ cups water

1½ cups defatted reduced-sodium chicken broth

¾ teaspoon salt

1 garlic clove, crushed

1 bay leaf, preferably imported

8 ounces small red potatoes, quartered

2 medium carrots, cut into ½-inch-thick slices

1 medium yellow bell pepper, diced

1 medium zucchini, diced

4 ounces fresh asparagus spears, diagonally sliced into 1-inch pieces

2 tablespoons cornstarch

¼ cup 1% low-fat milk

½ teaspoon dried tarragon

¼ teaspoon freshly ground black pepper

2 tablespoons chopped Italian parsley

½ teaspoon grated lemon zest

2 scallions, thinly sliced

The most delicate stews in French cuisine are called *blanquettes*, which means that the meat (usually veal or chicken) is not browned, but simply simmered in a light stock that is later enriched with eggs and cream. This stew has the pale delicacy of a blanquette, but the high-fat finishing touches are omitted.

1 In a large saucepan, combine the chicken, water, broth, ¼ teaspoon of the salt, the garlic and bay leaf, and bring to a boil over high heat. Reduce the heat to medium and simmer, uncovered, for 20 minutes, or until the chicken is just tender, skimming off the surface foam occasionally. With a slotted spoon, transfer the chicken to a medium bowl and cover loosely to keep warm.

2 Increase the heat to high and return the broth to a boil. Add the potatoes and carrots, and cook for 7 minutes. Add the bell peppers, zucchini and asparagus, and cook for 2 minutes, or until the vegetables are just tender. With a slotted spoon, transfer the vegetables to the bowl with the chicken; let the broth continue to boil.

3 In a small bowl, whisk together the cornstarch and milk. Whisk the milk mixture into the broth. Add the tarragon, black pepper and remaining ½ teaspoon salt, and return to a boil. Reduce the heat to medium-low and simmer for 1 minute.

4 Return the chicken and vegetables to the saucepan. Add the parsley and lemon zest, and stir to combine. Simmer for 2 minutes, or until heated through. Sprinkle the scallions over the stew and serve.

Preparation time 30 minutes • **Total time** 40 minutes • **Per serving** 291 calories, 5.1 g. fat (16% of calories), 1.3 g. saturated fat, 105 mg. cholesterol, 798 mg. sodium, 3.2 g. dietary fiber, 78 mg. calcium, 3 mg. iron, 49 mg. vitamin C, 6.5 mg. beta-carotene • **Serves 4**

❦ ❦ ❦

SUBSTITUTION
If dark meat doesn't find favor with your family, use bone-in chicken breast halves instead of a cut-up whole chicken. Cut the breasts in half crosswise for easy-to-serve pieces.

ON THE MENU
Start off the meal with a salad of dark, flavorful greens, such as arugula or watercress, tossed with a lively mustard vinaigrette. Complete the meal with juicy peaches and crisp rolled wafer cookies.

BASIL MINESTRONE

1 tablespoon olive oil

2 cups peeled, diced all-purpose potatoes

2 cups diced celery

1 medium onion, chopped

2 garlic cloves, minced

2 cups diced carrots

1½ cups defatted reduced-sodium chicken broth

1½ cups water

1 strip (2 inches long) lemon zest

1 bay leaf, preferably imported

½ teaspoon dried rosemary

½ teaspoon dried thyme

¼ teaspoon salt

¼ teaspoon freshly ground black pepper

1 cup diced zucchini

4 ounces green beans, cut into ½-inch pieces

1 can (14½ ounces) diced tomatoes with juice

1 can (10 ounces) cannellini beans, rinsed and drained

½ cup loosely packed fresh basil leaves, slivered

1 ounce Parmesan cheese, coarsely grated (optional)

Minestrone means "big soup," which suggests that all kinds of good things can go into this Italian favorite. The basics are dried beans, vegetables and pasta or rice—a combination that makes for hearty eating.

1 In a large saucepan, warm the oil over medium heat. Add the potatoes, celery and onions, and cook, stirring occasionally, for 5 minutes, or until the vegetables begin to soften. Stir in the garlic and cook for 30 seconds, or until fragrant.

2 Add the carrots, broth, water, lemon zest, bay leaf, rosemary, thyme, salt and black pepper; increase the heat to high and bring to a boil. Reduce the heat to medium-low and simmer, uncovered, for 10 minutes, or until the vegetables are tender. Stir in the zucchini and green beans, and cook for 5 minutes longer.

3 Stir in the tomatoes and their juice and the cannellini beans, and return to a boil over high heat. Reduce the heat to medium-low and simmer for 5 minutes. Stir in ¼ cup of the basil. Ladle the soup into 4 bowls and sprinkle with the remaining ¼ cup basil, and the Parmesan, if desired.

Preparation time 30 minutes • **Total time** 50 minutes • **Per serving** 242 calories, 4.6 g. fat (17% of calories), 0.6 g. saturated fat, 0 mg. cholesterol, 714 mg. sodium, 9 g. dietary fiber, 193 mg. calcium, 5 mg. iron, 54 mg. vitamin C, 10.1 mg. beta-carotene • **Serves 4**

❧ ❧ ❧

To sliver the basil leaves, first stack them, then roll them together.

Holding the roll of leaves, slice them crosswise so the leaves fall into slivers.

Hearty Borscht with Chicken

2 teaspoons olive oil

12 ounces skinless, boneless chicken thighs

3 medium carrots, sliced

1 large onion, diced

2 celery stalks, diced

2 garlic cloves, minced

2½ cups water

1 can (14½ ounces) diced tomatoes with juice

1 cup defatted reduced-sodium chicken broth

1 bay leaf, preferably imported

2 whole cloves

¼ teaspoon salt

¼ teaspoon freshly ground black pepper

2 cups diced red cabbage

2 cans (14½ ounces each) sliced beets, drained and cut into ½-inch-wide pieces

8 ounces all-purpose potatoes, diced

2 tablespoons red wine vinegar

¼ cup chopped fresh dill

½ cup reduced-fat sour cream or low-fat yogurt

Most Americans know borscht as a summery chilled beet soup they can buy in a jar. But in Eastern Europe, where borscht originated, it's more often a sustaining winter dish in which the beets are accompanied by a number of other vegetables and often pork and sausage. Potatoes, tomatoes, cabbage, carrots and chicken make this version a filling but low-fat meal-in-a-bowl.

1 In a large, heavy saucepan, warm the oil over medium-high heat until very hot but not smoking. Sauté the chicken for 4 minutes, or until browned on all sides. Reduce the heat to medium.

2 Stir in the carrots, onions, celery and garlic. Cover and cook for 5 minutes, or until the vegetables are just tender. Stir in the water, tomatoes and their juice, broth, bay leaf, cloves, salt and black pepper; increase the heat to high and bring the soup to a boil.

3 Stir in the cabbage, beets and potatoes. Reduce the heat to medium-low, cover and simmer for 20 minutes, or until the vegetables are tender. Stir in the vinegar and 2 tablespoons of the dill; remove the soup from the heat.

4 With tongs, remove the chicken from the soup and transfer to a plate. Allow the chicken to cool for about 5 minutes, then tear it into bite-size pieces and return to the pan.

5 Ladle the soup into 4 bowls and serve topped with the sour cream or yogurt and the remaining 2 tablespoons dill.

Preparation time 25 minutes • **Total time** 45 minutes • **Per serving** 346 calories, 10.4 g. fat (27% of calories), 3.3 g. saturated fat, 81 mg. cholesterol, 915 mg. sodium, 7.7 g. dietary fiber, 137 mg. calcium, 6 mg. iron, 64 mg. vitamin C, 9.6 mg. beta-carotene • **Serves 4**

❧ ❧ ❧

MAKE AHEAD
You can prepare the soup ahead of time through Step 4, then cover and refrigerate it. Remove any fat that has congealed at the top, reheat the soup and top with sour cream or yogurt and dill.

MARKET NOTE
Unlike some canned vegetables, canned beets retain most of the flavor and nutritional value of the fresh cooked vegetable. They do, however, lose some of their vitamin C and folacin in processing.

EIGHT-VEGETABLE CURRY

1 tablespoon plus 1 teaspoon olive oil

1 tablespoon curry powder

2 teaspoons ground cumin

1 teaspoon ground coriander

1 large onion, chopped

3 medium carrots, cut into 1-inch pieces

2 celery stalks, cut into 1-inch pieces

3 medium all-purpose potatoes, cut into 1-inch chunks

12 ounces butternut squash, peeled and cut into 1-inch chunks

2 garlic cloves, minced

1 large fresh jalapeño pepper, seeded and minced

1 bay leaf, preferably imported

¼ teaspoon salt

1½ cups defatted reduced-sodium chicken broth

1 cup water

2 cups small cauliflower florets

1 cup frozen peas

1 cup plain low-fat yogurt

¼ cup chopped fresh cilantro

Pinch of ground red pepper

Just about any vegetable you can think of could go into a curry, but a meatless curry tastes better made with dense, starchy vegetables. Potatoes, carrots and winter squash give this dish satisfying depth, and they absorb the seasonings beautifully. Acorn squash or pumpkin could stand in for the butternut squash; however, butternut is the easiest to peel and cut up.

1 In a large, heavy saucepan, warm the oil over medium-low heat. Add the curry powder, cumin and coriander, and cook, stirring, for 30 seconds, or until fragrant. Add the onions, carrots and celery; cover and cook for 10 minutes, stirring occasionally, until the vegetables begin to brown. Add the potatoes and cook, covered, for 5 minutes. Add the squash, garlic, jalapeño, bay leaf and salt, and cook, covered, for 5 minutes longer.

2 Stir the broth and water into the vegetable mixture; increase the heat to high and bring to a boil. Reduce the heat to medium and simmer, uncovered, for 10 minutes.

3 Add the cauliflower and simmer, uncovered, for 5 minutes. Add the peas and cook for 3 minutes longer, or until all the vegetables are tender.

4 Meanwhile, in a small bowl, whisk together the yogurt, cilantro and ground red pepper.

5 Ladle the curry into 4 bowls and top with the yogurt mixture.

Preparation time 35 minutes • **Total time** 55 minutes • **Per serving** 317 calories, 6.4 g. fat (18% of calories), 1.3 g. saturated fat, 3 mg. cholesterol, 516 mg. sodium, 9.4 g. dietary fiber, 229 mg. calcium, 4 mg. iron, 106 mg. vitamin C, 12.7 mg. beta-carotene • **Serves 4**

❧ ❧ ❧

ON THE MENU
Indian basmati rice is the perfect complement to any curry. This fragrant long-grain rice has a deliciously nutlike fragrance and flavor. As an alternative, try Texmati and Calmati, American rice varieties that taste similar to basmati but are grown in Texas and California, respectively. After opening the package, transfer basmati rice to an airtight container.

SEAFOOD CHOWDER WITH GARLIC TOASTS

1 tablespoon olive oil

1 medium onion, chopped

2 celery stalks, diced

¼ cup chopped shallots or onion

1 bay leaf, preferably imported

¼ teaspoon fennel seeds, crushed

2 tablespoons all-purpose flour

½ cup white wine

12 ounces small red potatoes, diced

1½ cups sliced carrots, cut
     ½-inch thick

1½ cups defatted reduced-sodium
     chicken broth

1½ cups water

½ cup 1% low-fat milk

½ teaspoon dried thyme

¼ teaspoon salt

¼ teaspoon freshly ground
     black pepper

8 slices crusty French bread, cut
     ½-inch thick (about 4 ounces
     total)

1 garlic clove, halved

8 ounces cod fillet, cut into
     chunks

4 ounces medium shrimp, peeled
     and deveined, with tails attached

¼ cup chopped Italian parsley

Because seafood cooks in so little time (and you don't have to brown fish or shellfish before simmering it), chowders are quicker to make than meat stews. This chowder calls for cod and shrimp, readily available everywhere in the country. A touch of anise flavor, in the form of crushed fennel seeds, is reminiscent of French bouillabaisse, which often contains anise liqueur. The garlicky toasts served with the chowder are another classic French touch.

1 In a large saucepan, warm the oil over medium-low heat. Add the onions, celery, shallots or onions, bay leaf and fennel seeds; cover and cook, stirring occasionally, for about 5 minutes, or until the vegetables begin to soften.

2 Add the flour and cook, stirring, for 2 minutes. Stir in the wine, increase the heat to high and bring to a boil. Boil for 1 minute.

3 Add the potatoes, carrots, broth, water, milk, thyme, salt and black pepper, and bring to a boil. Reduce the heat to medium-low, cover and simmer for 15 minutes, or until the vegetables are tender.

4 Meanwhile, preheat the broiler. Toast the bread 5 to 6 inches from the heat for about 1 minute per side, or until lightly browned. Rub the toasted bread with the cut sides of the garlic clove; set aside.

5 Add the cod and shrimp to the soup. Cover and simmer for 4 to 5 minutes, or until the seafood turns opaque.

6 Ladle the soup into 4 bowls and serve each with 2 pieces of toasted bread. Sprinkle with the parsley.

Preparation time 35 minutes • **Total time** 45 minutes • **Per serving** 349 calories, 5.7 g. fat (15% of calories), 1 g. saturated fat, 61 mg. cholesterol, 674 mg. sodium, 4.9 g. dietary fiber, 129 mg. calcium, 3 mg. iron, 26 mg. vitamin C, 7.2 mg. beta-carotene • **Serves 4**

❧ ❧ ❧

SUBSTITUTION
As with many fish recipes, it's possible to replace the cod with another similarly textured fish, such as pollack or haddock.

MARKET AND PANTRY
French bread should be kept in a paper bag; if stored in a plastic bag, its crust will become soggy and tough.

Moroccan Lentil and Chick-Pea Soup

1 tablespoon plus 1 teaspoon olive oil

1 cup finely chopped onions

4 medium carrots, finely chopped

2 celery stalks, finely chopped

3 garlic cloves, minced

2 teaspoons grated fresh ginger

2 teaspoons ground cumin

½ teaspoon dried thyme

½ teaspoon ground turmeric

Pinch of ground cloves

8 ounces lentils, picked over and rinsed

2 cups defatted reduced-sodium chicken broth

1 can (14½ ounces) diced tomatoes with juice

3 cups water

1 bay leaf, preferably imported

½ teaspoon freshly ground black pepper

¼ teaspoon salt

1 can (10 ounces) chick-peas, rinsed and drained

¼ cup chopped fresh cilantro

Some culinary historians hold that highly spiced cuisines develop in hot climates because heat deadens hunger; spicy food, which piques the appetite, thus becomes almost a necessity for survival. Moroccan cuisine is often spicy, combining seasonings we think of as "sweet"—cloves, cinnamon and nutmeg, for instance—with savory garlic and herbs, meats, grains and legumes.

1 In a large, heavy saucepan, warm the oil over medium-high heat. Add the onions, carrots and celery; cover and cook, stirring frequently, for 5 minutes, or until the vegetables are tender. Stir in the garlic, ginger, cumin, thyme, turmeric and cloves, and cook for 30 seconds, or until fragrant.

2 Add the lentils, broth, tomatoes and their juice, water, bay leaf, black pepper and salt. Increase the heat to high and bring to a boil. Reduce the heat to medium, cover and simmer for 30 to 40 minutes, or until the lentils are tender.

3 Stir in the the chick-peas and simmer for 2 minutes, or until heated through. Just before serving, stir in the cilantro.

Preparation time 30 minutes • **Total time** 1 hour 10 minutes • **Per serving** 369 calories, 6.9 g. fat (17% of calories), 0.8 g. saturated fat, 0 mg. cholesterol, 755 mg. sodium, 12.5 g. dietary fiber, 128 mg. calcium, 8 mg. iron, 31 mg. vitamin C, 12.6 mg. beta-carotene • **Serves 4**

Brownish green lentils are those most commonly found in supermarkets. Like all lentils, they need no presoaking. This type cooks in 30 to 40 minutes.

Red lentils, sold in health-food stores and gourmet shops, cook more quickly—in 20 to 30 minutes. Use them in this recipe if you prefer.

CINCINNATI TURKEY CHILI

1 tablespoon plus 1 teaspoon vegetable oil

12 ounces skinless, boneless turkey breast, cut into 1-inch cubes

1 medium yellow onion, finely chopped

1 medium green bell pepper, diced

3 garlic cloves, minced

4 teaspoons chili powder

2 teaspoons ground cumin

1 teaspoon dried oregano

½ teaspoon ground cinnamon

1 can (28 ounces) crushed tomatoes with juice

¾ cup defatted reduced-sodium chicken broth

2 cans (19 ounces each) red kidney beans, rinsed and drained

1 teaspoon red wine vinegar

½ teaspoon Worcestershire sauce

6 ounces spaghetti

¼ cup finely chopped red onion

2 ounces reduced-fat sharp Cheddar cheese, finely grated

½ cup oyster crackers (optional)

Cincinnati's famed chili is in a class by itself. Its seasonings, including cinnamon and cloves, support the theory that the dish was devised by Greek immigrants. Served atop a mound of spaghetti, this chili may have been the first "have it your way" food. In a code peculiar to the dish, you order it "three-way" (the spaghetti and chili topped with shredded Cheddar); "four-way" (with cheese plus chopped raw onions); or "five-way" (crowned with Cheddar, onions and kidney beans). This five-way turkey chili—here the beans are cooked right in the chili—is served with oyster crackers, a traditional, if surprising, accompaniment.

1 Bring a large covered pot of water to a boil over high heat.

2 Meanwhile, in a large, heavy saucepan, warm the oil over medium-high heat until very hot but not smoking. Sauté the turkey for 2 to 3 minutes, or until browned; transfer the turkey to a plate.

3 Add the yellow onions and bell peppers to the pan. Reduce the heat to medium, cover and cook, stirring occasionally, for 5 minutes, or until the vegetables are tender. Add the garlic, chili powder, cumin, oregano and cinnamon, and stir for 30 seconds, or until fragrant.

4 Add the tomatoes and their juice, and the broth, and bring to a boil. Add the beans, vinegar and Worcestershire, and bring to a boil. Reduce the heat to medium-low, cover and simmer for 10 minutes. Add the turkey and simmer for 5 minutes longer.

5 While the chili is simmering, add the spaghetti to the boiling water, return to a boil and cook for 10 to 12 minutes, or according to package directions until al dente. Drain the spaghetti in a colander.

6 Divide the spaghetti among 4 bowls. Ladle the chili over the spaghetti and top with the red onions and Cheddar. Serve with oyster crackers, if desired.

Preparation time 25 minutes • **Total time** 40 minutes • **Per serving** 608 calories, 11 g. fat (16% of calories), 2.8 g. saturated fat, 63 mg. cholesterol, 971 mg. sodium, 15.4 g. dietary fiber, 295 mg. calcium, 8 mg. iron, 55 mg. vitamin C, 1.4 mg. beta-carotene • **Serves 4**

MEXICAN TURKEY MEATBALL SOUP

3 garlic cloves, crushed

1 large fresh jalapeño pepper, seeded and coarsely chopped

12 ounces skinless, boneless turkey breast, cut into chunks

1 cup fresh breadcrumbs

2 large egg whites, lightly beaten

¼ cup chopped fresh cilantro

1½ teaspoons ground cumin

¼ teaspoon salt

1 tablespoon vegetable oil

1 medium onion, finely chopped

2 medium carrots, thinly sliced

2 celery stalks, finely chopped

8 ounces medium white mushrooms, sliced

1 can (35 ounces) whole Italian tomatoes, drained and coarsely chopped, with juice reserved

1½ cups defatted reduced-sodium chicken broth

1½ cups water

½ teaspoon freshly ground black pepper

1 cup frozen corn kernels

½ medium avocado, diced

Cilantro leaves, for garnish (optional)

*S*opa de albóndigas—that's the Mexican term for meatball soup. Garlic, jalapeño, cilantro and cumin give the low-fat turkey meatballs real Mexican flavor; the corn in the soup and the avocado garnish are also south-of-the-border touches. Fresh breadcrumbs make the meatballs light: On page 87, you'll find directions for making your own fresh breadcrumbs.

1 In a food processor, combine the garlic and jalapeño, and process just until minced; transfer 1 tablespoon of the mixture to a cup.

2 Add the turkey to the processor and process until finely ground.

3 Add the breadcrumbs, egg whites, chopped cilantro, cumin and ⅛ teaspoon of the salt, and pulse just until blended. Shape the mixture into twelve to sixteen 1½- to 2-inch meatballs; set aside.

4 In a large saucepan, warm the oil over medium heat. Add the onions, carrots, celery and reserved 1 tablespoon jalapeño-garlic mixture; cover and cook for 4 to 5 minutes, or until the vegetables begin to soften. Stir in the mushrooms and cook for 2 minutes longer.

5 Stir in the tomatoes and their juice, the broth, water, black pepper and remaining ⅛ teaspoon salt. Increase the heat to high and bring to a boil. Add the meatballs and return to a boil. Reduce the heat to medium-low, cover and simmer the soup for 10 minutes.

6 Add the corn and simmer for 2 minutes longer. Spoon the meatball soup into 4 bowls and top each portion with some diced avocado. Garnish with cilantro leaves, if desired.

Preparation time 35 minutes • **Total time** 50 minutes • **Per serving** 354 calories, 9.7 g. fat (25% of calories), 1.5 g. saturated fat, 53 mg. cholesterol, 946 mg. sodium, 6.6 g. dietary fiber, 135 mg. calcium, 5 mg. iron, 64 mg. vitamin C, 7.2 mg. beta-carotene • **Serves 4**

❧ ❧ ❧

FOR A CHANGE
When fresh corn is plentiful, you can slice the kernels off a few cobs to use instead of the frozen corn.

NUTRITION NOTE
Smooth-skinned green Florida avocados contain about half the fat of California's black-skinned Haas and Fuerte avocados.

LAMB AND VEGETABLE STEW

12 ounces lean, well-trimmed boneless leg of lamb, cut into ¾-inch chunks

½ teaspoon salt

¼ teaspoon freshly ground black pepper

1 tablespoon plus 1 teaspoon olive oil

1 medium onion, chopped

2 celery stalks, diced

3 garlic cloves, minced

2 teaspoons ground coriander

2 teaspoons ground cumin

1 teaspoon dried oregano

½ teaspoon dried thyme

1 bay leaf, preferably imported

1 can (35 ounces) whole tomatoes, drained and chopped, with juice reserved

½ cup defatted reduced-sodium chicken broth

1 pound all-purpose potatoes, peeled and cut into 2 x ½-inch pieces

½ pound carrots, cut into 2 x ½-inch pieces

1 cup frozen lima beans

¼ cup chopped Italian parsley

For a bit of a change—and to cut a traditionally long cooking time—the carrots and potatoes that go into this stew are cut into thick sticks rather than cubes. Thin-skinned long white potatoes (one variety is called White Rose) are best for this recipe; starchy baking potatoes such as Russets will fall apart if cooked in this fashion.

1 In a medium bowl, toss the lamb with ¼ teaspoon of the salt and the black pepper. In a large, heavy saucepan, warm the oil over medium-high heat until very hot but not smoking. Sauté the lamb for 2 minutes, or until browned on all sides.

2 Reduce the heat to medium and stir in the onions and celery. Cover and cook, stirring occasionally, for 5 minutes, or until the vegetables begin to soften. Stir in the garlic, coriander, cumin, oregano, thyme and bay leaf, and cook for 30 seconds, or until fragrant. Add the tomatoes and their juice, the broth and remaining ¼ teaspoon salt. Reduce the heat to medium-low and simmer, covered, for 20 minutes.

3 Stir in the potatoes, carrots and lima beans, and simmer, uncovered, for 20 minutes longer, or until the meat and vegetables are tender. Just before serving, sprinkle with the parsley.

Preparation time 20 minutes • **Total time** 1 hour 10 minutes • **Per serving** 365 calories, 9.6 g. fat (24% of calories), 2.1 g. saturated fat, 54 mg. cholesterol, 882 mg. sodium, 8.7 g. dietary fiber, 150 mg. calcium, 6 mg. iron, 76 mg. vitamin C, 10.7 mg. beta-carotene • **Serves 4**

❧ ❧ ❧

HEAD START
Chop and dice the onion and celery, and combine them in a tightly sealed bag; cut up the potatoes and carrots, and combine them in a second bag; measure out the coriander, cumin, oregano and thyme, and seal the mixture in a twist of foil.

MAKE AHEAD
You can cook the stew a day ahead of time, then reheat it before serving. Add the parsley at the last minute. You can also freeze the stew (in individual portions for convenience, if you like), but the potatoes may be a bit mushy when you thaw and reheat it.

NUTRITION NOTE
Lima beans, like most legumes, are an excellent low-fat source of protein, iron and dietary fiber. Use either baby limas or meaty Fordhooks for this recipe.

Satisfying Oven Dinners

❧ ❧ ❧

CASSEROLES, PASTAS AND POT PIE—

OLD FAVORITES AND

NEW DELIGHTS

FROM THE OVEN

TEX-MEX ARROZ CON POLLO

2 teaspoons olive oil

1 large red bell pepper, diced

1 medium onion, diced

2 celery stalks, diced

3 garlic cloves, minced

1 bay leaf, preferably imported

12 ounces skinless, boneless chicken thighs, cut into 2-inch chunks

¾ cup long-grain white rice

2 teaspoons chili powder

2 teaspoons ground cumin

1 teaspoon dried oregano

½ teaspoon ground turmeric

⅛ teaspoon ground red pepper

1 cup defatted reduced-sodium chicken broth

½ cup water

1 can (4 ounces) chopped green chilies, drained

1 can (15 ounces) black beans, rinsed and drained

½ cup diced tomato

Fresh cilantro or parsley sprigs and lemon slices, for garnish (optional)

Spanish in origin, *arroz con pollo* (literally "chicken with rice") is a down-to-earth version of the lavish party dish called *paella* (saffron-tinted rice with shellfish, sausage, chicken and vegetables). Simpler but no less delicious, this Mexican-influenced arroz con pollo is made with hearty black beans—*frijoles negros*—and green chilies; the typically Tex-Mex seasonings include chili powder, garlic, cumin and oregano.

1 Preheat the oven to 375°.

2 In a Dutch oven or large ovenproof saucepan, warm the oil over medium-high heat. Add the bell peppers, onions, celery, garlic and bay leaf, and sauté for 2 to 3 minutes, or until the vegetables begin to soften. Add the chicken, reduce the heat to medium and sauté for 3 minutes, or until the chicken is lightly browned. Stir in the rice, chili powder, cumin, oregano, turmeric and ground red pepper, and cook for 1 minute, or until the spices are fragrant.

3 Stir in the broth, water and green chilies, and bring to a boil over medium-high heat. Cover the pan tightly and bake for 20 minutes.

4 Uncover the pan and stir in the black beans and tomatoes. Bake, uncovered, for 5 minutes longer, or until the beans are heated through. Garnish with cilantro or parsley sprigs and lemon slices, if desired.

Preparation time 20 minutes • **Total time** 1 hour • **Per serving** 363 calories, 7 g. fat (17% of calories), 1.3 g. saturated fat, 71 mg. cholesterol, 617 mg. sodium, 5.7 g. dietary fiber, 86 mg. calcium, 5 mg. iron, 81 mg. vitamin C, 1.4 mg. beta-carotene • **Serves 4**

❧ ❧ ❧

FOOD FACT
The orangy-yellow spice turmeric gives the rice in this recipe a golden color (saffron, which costs much more than turmeric, is often used for this purpose in Spanish dishes). Ground turmeric is produced by drying and then grinding a root-like rhizome that resembles gingerroot. Turmeric is found in curry powder and in prepared mustard.

Preceding pages: Turkey and Rice Stuffed Peppers (recipe on page 52).

SPICE-RUBBED COD WITH VEGETABLES

1½ pounds cod fillet, in one piece (1 inch thick)

1 teaspoon ground cumin

½ teaspoon ground ginger

½ teaspoon salt

¼ teaspoon paprika

Pinch of ground red pepper

1 tablespoon plus 1 teaspoon extra-virgin olive oil

1½ pounds small red potatoes, quartered

4 medium carrots, cut diagonally into ¼-inch-thick slices

12 ounces green beans, trimmed

12 ounces yellow squash, cut diagonally into ¼-inch-thick slices

¼ teaspoon freshly ground black pepper

¼ cup chopped fresh cilantro

2 scallions, thinly sliced

You know how to roast turkey and chicken, beef and pork—now try roasting a thick fish fillet. Here cod fillet is rubbed with a cumin-based spice mixture and roasted on a bed of potatoes, carrots, summer squash and green beans. Because the fish cooks in such a short time, some of the vegetables are briefly parboiled so that they will be done as quickly as the cod.

1 Preheat the oven to 425°.

2 Line a baking sheet with foil. Place the fish on the prepared baking sheet. In a small bowl, combine the cumin, ginger, ¼ teaspoon of the salt, the paprika and ground red pepper. Stir in 2 teaspoons of the oil. Brush both sides of the fish with the seasoned oil. Cover the fish loosely and refrigerate while you prepare the vegetables.

3 Place the potatoes in a large saucepan and add water to cover; bring to a boil over high heat. Reduce the heat to medium, cover and simmer for 5 minutes. Add the carrots, cover and cook for 2 minutes. Add the green beans and cook, uncovered, for 1 minute. Drain the vegetables in a colander.

4 Transfer the drained vegetables to a large bowl and add the squash, black pepper and the remaining 2 teaspoons oil and ¼ teaspoon salt; toss to combine. Spread the vegetables out in a single layer in a jelly-roll pan and bake for 15 minutes.

5 Place the fish on top of the vegetables and bake for 10 to 15 minutes longer, or until the fish just flakes when tested with a knife and the vegetables are tender. Transfer the fish and vegetables to a warmed platter and scatter the cilantro and scallions over the fish and vegetables.

Preparation time 20 minutes • **Total time** 1 hour • **Per serving** 393 calories, 6.7 g. fat (15% of calories), 1 g. saturated fat, 73 mg. cholesterol, 412 mg. sodium, 7.6 g. dietary fiber, 106 mg. calcium, 4 mg. iron, 56 mg. vitamin C, 12.8 mg. beta-carotene • **Serves 4**

❧ ❧ ❧

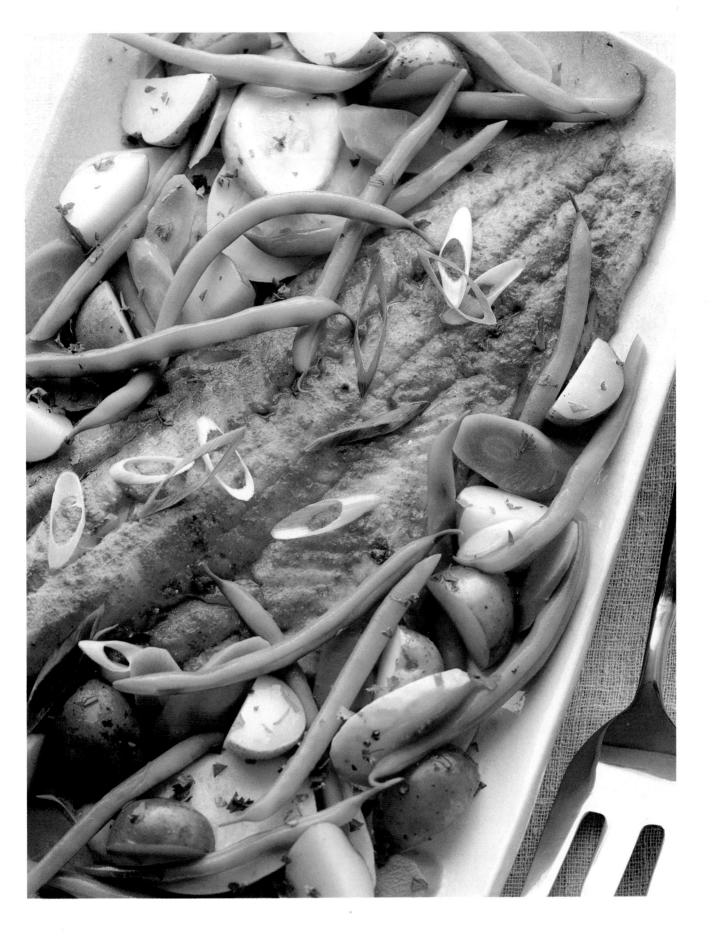

MEDITERRANEAN SHRIMP WITH FETA

1 pound all-purpose potatoes, peeled and thinly sliced

8 ounces green beans, trimmed and halved diagonally

1 medium zucchini, halved lengthwise and thinly sliced

2 teaspoons olive oil

1 medium onion, thinly sliced

1 red bell pepper, coarsely chopped

2 garlic cloves, minced

1 can (28 ounces) crushed tomatoes with juice

1 pound medium shrimp, peeled and deveined, with tails attached

¼ cup dry white wine

½ teaspoon dried oregano

½ teaspoon salt

¼ teaspoon freshly ground black pepper

2 ounces feta cheese, crumbled

3 tablespoons chopped Italian parsley

The Greek islands are, naturally enough, the home of some exceptional seafood cookery. This is a favorite Greek way of preparing shrimp—the shellfish Americans love best. The potatoes are not a traditional component of this dish, but they make substantial fare of what might otherwise be a very light meal.

1 Preheat the oven to 375°.

2 Place the potatoes in a large saucepan and add water to cover. Bring to a boil and cook for 7 minutes. Add the green beans and zucchini, and cook for 3 minutes longer. Drain the vegetables in a colander and transfer to a large bowl.

3 Meanwhile, in a medium no-stick skillet, warm the oil over medium heat. Add the onions, bell peppers and garlic, and cook for 3 minutes, or until softened. Add the onion mixture to the bowl with the other vegetables.

4 Add the tomatoes and their juice, the shrimp, wine, oregano, salt and black pepper to the vegetables, and toss to combine. Transfer the mixture to an 11 x 7-inch baking dish, cover with foil and bake for 25 minutes.

5 Uncover the dish and sprinkle the feta on top. Bake, uncovered, for 3 minutes longer.

6 Remove the dish from the oven and sprinkle with the parsley.

Preparation time 15 minutes • **Total time** 1 hour • **Per serving** 309 calories, 7.6 g. fat (22% of calories), 2.8 g. saturated fat, 152 mg. cholesterol, 904 mg. sodium, 5.2 g. dietary fiber, 223 mg. calcium, 5 mg. iron, 100 mg. vitamin C, 1.7 mg. beta-carotene • **Serves 4**

❧ ❧ ❧

MARKET AND PANTRY
If you prefer to purchase shelled shrimp, buy about 8 ounces instead of 1 pound of unshelled shrimp. Either way, you should get 30 to 35 medium shrimp.

ON THE MENU
Offer French or Italian bread—or warm pita pockets—with the shrimp. Finish with a fruit salad sweetened with honey and sprinkled lightly with cinnamon.

TURKEY AND RICE STUFFED PEPPERS

4 large red bell peppers plus
  1 small red bell pepper, or a
  mix of red and yellow peppers

2 cups water

½ cup long-grain white rice

¾ teaspoon salt

2 teaspoons olive oil

1 pound lean ground turkey

1 medium onion, chopped

2 garlic cloves, minced

1½ teaspoons dried thyme or
  1 teaspoon chopped fresh
  thyme

¼ teaspoon freshly ground black
  pepper

1 pound fresh spinach, stemmed
  and coarsely chopped

½ cup dried currants

¼ cup chopped parsley

To make sure the peppers stand upright in the pan, shave a thin slice off the bottoms of the peppers before blanching them.

Food served in edible containers—zucchini boats, melon bowls or these striking red bell pepper cups—always makes a fun meal. When you've eaten the filling, be sure to polish off your "dish" as well: Red bell peppers are a good source of vitamin C.

1 Preheat the oven to 350°. Bring a large saucepan of water to a boil over high heat.

2 Meanwhile, cut off and discard the tops of the 4 large bell peppers. Seed the large peppers, being careful not to puncture them. Seed and dice the small bell pepper; set aside.

3 Blanch the whole peppers in the boiling water for 2 minutes, or until slightly softened. Drain the peppers on paper towels, then stand the peppers upright in an 8 x 8-inch baking dish; set aside.

4 In a medium saucepan, combine 1 cup of the water, the rice and ¼ teaspoon of the salt. Cover and bring to a boil over medium-high heat; reduce the heat to medium and cook, covered, for 15 to 17 minutes, or until the rice is tender and the liquid is absorbed.

5 Meanwhile, in a large no-stick skillet, warm the oil over medium-high heat until hot but not smoking. Add the turkey and sauté for about 3 minutes, breaking up any clumps with a spoon. Add the onions, garlic, thyme, black pepper and remaining ½ teaspoon salt, and cook for about 3 minutes, or until the onions are softened.

6 Add the diced bell peppers, spinach, currants and parsley; cover and cook for 3 minutes, or until the spinach is wilted. Remove the pan from the heat.

7 Fluff the cooked rice with a fork. Add the spinach mixture to the rice and stir to combine. Spoon the rice mixture into the bell peppers, pour the remaining 1 cup water into the baking dish around the peppers and bake for 15 minutes, or until the peppers and filling are hot.

Preparation time 15 minutes • **Total time** 1 hour • **Per serving** 386 calories, 11.5 g. fat (27% of calories), 2.7 g. saturated fat, 83 mg. cholesterol, 591 mg. sodium, 6 g. dietary fiber, 157 mg. calcium, 7 mg. iron, 246 mg. vitamin C, 7.3 mg. beta-carotene • **Serves 4**

GARDEN LASAGNA

1 teaspoon vegetable oil

8 ounces eggplant, diced

½ cup chopped onion

1 large garlic clove, minced

¼ cup plus 1 tablespoon chopped fresh basil

½ teaspoon salt

¼ teaspoon freshly ground black pepper

1 can (16 ounces) crushed tomatoes with juice

3 medium carrots, diced

1¼ cups water

1 cup part-skim ricotta cheese

1 tablespoon grated Parmesan cheese

1 large egg white

6 uncooked no-boil lasagna noodles

2 ounces part-skim mozzarella cheese, grated

The Italians use the term *alla giardiniera*—meaning lady-gardener-style—to describe a dish made with plenty of fresh vegetables. The sauce for this lasagna alla giardiniera contains eggplant, onions, carrots and basil along with the usual tomatoes. A busy gardener (or any busy person) will appreciate no-boil lasagna noodles: They go right from the package into the casserole (you don't have to precook them) and absorb liquid as they bake. To ensure that the noodles soften completely, see that they are completely covered with sauce.

1 Preheat the oven to 375°. Spray an 8 x 8-inch baking dish with no-stick spray.

2 In a large no-stick skillet, warm the oil over medium-high heat. Add the eggplant, onions, garlic, 1 tablespoon of the basil, ¼ teaspoon of the salt and the black pepper, and sauté for 3 minutes. Add the tomatoes and their juice, the carrots and 1 cup of the water, and simmer for 5 minutes, or until the eggplant is tender.

3 While the sauce is simmering, in a medium bowl, combine the ricotta, Parmesan, egg white, and remaining ¼ cup basil and ¼ teaspoon salt; set aside.

4 Spoon one-third of the tomato sauce into the prepared baking dish. Lay 2 lasagna noodles over the sauce, then top with half the cheese mixture and 2 more noodles. Repeat, using half the remaining sauce and all the remaining noodles and cheese mixture. Spoon the remaining sauce on top and sprinkle with the mozzarella. Pour the remaining ¼ cup water into the baking dish, around the edges.

5 Cover the lasagna with foil and bake for 15 minutes; uncover the dish and bake for another 15 minutes, or until bubbly.

Preparation time 20 minutes • **Total time** 1 hour • **Per serving** 298 calories, 9.4 g. fat (28% of calories), 4.9 g. saturated fat, 28 mg. cholesterol, 662 mg. sodium, 4.4 g. dietary fiber, 379 mg. calcium, 3 mg. iron, 25 mg. vitamin C, 9.8 mg. beta-carotene • **Serves 4**

❧ ❧ ❧

PASTITSIO

1 cup 1% low-fat milk

½ cup defatted chicken broth

3 tablespoons all-purpose flour

3 tablespoons grated Parmesan cheese

¼ teaspoon nutmeg, preferably freshly grated

½ cup part-skim ricotta cheese

1 tablespoon chopped fresh dill

8 ounces fettuccine

12 ounces lean leg of lamb, cut into chunks

8 ounces eggplant, diced

8 ounces zucchini, diced

½ cup coarsely chopped onion

3 tablespoons chopped fresh mint

¼ teaspoon freshly ground black pepper

1 can (15 ounces) tomato sauce

A not-too-distant cousin of lasagna, *pastitsio* is a Greek pasta casserole with layers of macaroni, cheese sauce and meat. Rather than the traditional béchamel, this recipe is made with a ricotta-based sauce that's thick and rich-tasting, but low in fat. And, for a contemporary look, fettuccine is used instead of macaroni.

1 Preheat the oven to 375°. Bring a large covered pot of water to a boil over high heat.

2 Meanwhile, in a large no-stick skillet, whisk together the milk, broth, flour, 2 tablespoons of the Parmesan and the nutmeg over medium-high heat. Cook, whisking constantly, for 3 minutes, or until thickened. Whisk in the ricotta and dill, then transfer the mixture to a large bowl. Rinse and dry the skillet.

3 Add the noodles to the boiling water, return to a boil and cook for 6 to 7 minutes, or according to package directions until al dente. Drain the pasta in a colander, then add to the cheese mixture and toss well; set aside.

4 While the pasta is cooking, place the lamb chunks in a food processor and process until finely ground.

5 Place the lamb, eggplant, zucchini and onions in the large skillet, and cook over medium-high heat for 5 minutes, or until the vegetables are tender and the lamb is browned on all sides. Stir in the mint and black pepper. Stir in the tomato sauce and simmer, stirring occasionally, for 2 minutes. Remove the skillet from the heat.

6 Spray an 11 x 7-inch baking dish with no-stick spray. Spoon half of the pasta-cheese mixture into the bottom. Spoon the lamb mixture over the pasta and then top with the remaining pasta-cheese mixture. Bake for 10 minutes, then sprinkle with the remaining 1 tablespoon Parmesan. Bake for another 5 minutes, or until heated through.

Preparation time 20 minutes • **Total time** 1 hour • **Per serving** 501 calories, 11.3 g. fat (20% of calories), 4.6 g. saturated fat, 123 mg. cholesterol, 977 mg. sodium, 4.8 g. dietary fiber, 289 mg. calcium, 6 mg. iron, 23 mg. vitamin C, 1 mg. beta-carotene • **Serves 4**

❧ ❧ ❧

MOROCCAN CHICKEN POT PIE

2 cups water

1 cinnamon stick

4 whole cloves

¼ teaspoon ground turmeric

½ teaspoon salt

¼ teaspoon freshly ground black pepper

1 pound skinless, boneless chicken breast halves, cut into 1-inch cubes

1 pound carrots, diced

12 ounces all-purpose potatoes, peeled and diced

8 ounces small pearl onions, peeled and halved

1 tablespoon cornstarch dissolved in 3 tablespoons cold water

1 cup frozen peas, thawed

½ cup golden raisins

¼ cup chopped Italian parsley

2 tablespoons honey

1 tablespoon vegetable oil

1 tablespoon hot water

6 sheets phyllo dough

Rather than a heavy crust, this very deep-dish pie is topped with a light, crisp layer of phyllo—paper-thin Greek pastry sheets. Phyllo (or filo) is sold in most supermarkets. Keep it wrapped or covered with a damp towel during preparation.

1 Preheat the oven to 400°. In a large skillet, combine the 2 cups of water, the cinnamon stick, cloves, turmeric, ¼ teaspoon of the salt and ⅛ teaspoon of the black pepper. Add the chicken to the skillet and bring to a simmer over medium-high heat. Poach the chicken for 5 to 7 minutes, or until cooked through. Using a slotted spoon, transfer the chicken to a large bowl. Discard the cinnamon stick and cloves.

2 Add the carrots, potatoes and onions to the skillet, and cook for about 8 minutes, or until the vegetables are tender. Using a slotted spoon, transfer the vegetables to the bowl with the chicken.

3 Pour off all but ¼ cup of the liquid from the skillet. Stir the cornstarch mixture to recombine it, then add it to the skillet. Cook, stirring, over medium-high heat for 1 minute, or until the sauce is slightly thickened. Pour the sauce over the chicken and vegetables, then add the peas, raisins, parsley, and remaining ¼ teaspoon salt and ⅛ teaspoon black pepper. Toss gently but thoroughly to combine. Spoon the chicken mixture into a 1½-quart soufflé dish or casserole; set aside.

4 In a small bowl, whisk together the honey, oil and hot water. Place the stacked sheets of phyllo on a work surface and cover with a damp towel. Remove 1 sheet from the stack and place it on the work surface; brush lightly with the honey mixture. Place a second sheet on top of the first and brush with the honey mixture. Continue in this manner for all 6 sheets (don't worry if the sheets stick together). Place the phyllo stack on top of the soufflé dish or casserole, tucking under the edges if necessary for fit. Brush the top with any remaining honey mixture.

5 Bake the pot pie for 15 minutes, or until the crust is golden.

Preparation time 20 minutes • **Total time** 1 hour • **Per serving** 485 calories, 7.1 g. fat (13% of calories), 1.1 g. saturated fat, 66 mg. cholesterol, 579 mg. sodium, 7.2 g. dietary fiber, 101 mg. calcium, 4 mg. iron, 40 mg. vitamin C, 19.5 mg. beta-carotene • **Serves 4**

❧ ❧ ❧

SALMON AND VEGETABLE PACKETS

1 tablespoon olive oil

2 medium carrots, cut into
   julienne strips

2 small leeks, white part only, well
   washed and sliced ¼ inch thick

2 small zucchini, halved and thinly
   sliced lengthwise

2 medium tomatoes, seeded and
   diced

⅓ cup minced shallots

2 tablespoons chopped Italian
   parsley

½ teaspoon grated fresh ginger

¼ teaspoon freshly ground black
   pepper

⅛ teaspoon salt

4 salmon fillets (4 ounces each),
   skinned

2 tablespoons dry sherry

2 tablespoons reduced-sodium
   soy sauce

1 teaspoon honey

6 ounces orzo pasta

Foil packets make it a snap to poach individual portions of salmon along with a medley of vegetables. If you prefer to make the packets out of parchment paper rather than foil, see Steps 1 and 4 of the recipe for Turkey Primavera in Parchment (page 67).

1 Preheat the oven to 425°. Bring a large covered pot of water and a large covered saucepan of water to a boil over high heat. Meanwhile, cut four 17 x 12-inch sheets of foil. Brush the sheets of foil lightly with the oil.

2 Add the carrots, leeks and zucchini to the saucepan of boiling water, and cook for 3 minutes. Drain the vegetables in a colander and rinse under cold running water; drain again. Transfer the vegetables to a medium bowl and toss with the tomatoes, shallots, parsley and ginger.

3 Spoon the vegetables evenly onto one end of each piece of foil; sprinkle with the pepper and salt. Place each fillet on top of a portion of vegetables.

4 In a small bowl, stir together the sherry, soy sauce and honey. Drizzle this mixture evenly over the fish and vegetables, then fold the foil over the contents, sealing the edges together with small folds.

5 Place the packets on a baking sheet and bake for 15 minutes, or until the fish just flakes when tested with a fork (open one packet to check).

6 While the fish is baking, add the pasta to the boiling water in the large pot, return to a boil and cook for 6 to 7 minutes, or according to package directions until al dente. Drain in a colander.

7 Divide the pasta among 4 plates. Open the packets, remove the fish and vegetables and arrange on top of each serving of pasta. Pour any cooking juices left in the packets over the fish and vegetables.

Preparation time 30 minutes • **Total time** 55 minutes • **Per serving** 441 calories, 11.7 g. fat (24% of calories), 1.7 g. saturated fat, 62 mg. cholesterol, 453 mg. sodium, 4 g. dietary fiber, 78 mg. calcium, 5 mg. iron, 28 mg. vitamin C, 6.5 mg. beta-carotene
Serves 4

❧ ❧ ❧

VEGETARIAN SHEPHERD'S PIE

1½ pounds small unpeeled all-purpose potatoes, cut into 1-inch cubes

1 cup canned black beans, rinsed and drained

1 cup canned kidney beans, rinsed and drained

1 can (15 ounces) no-salt-added tomato sauce

1 cup chopped onion

2 garlic cloves, minced

½ teaspoon salt

½ teaspoon freshly ground black pepper

½ cup 1% low-fat milk

2 tablespoons unsalted butter or margarine

2 tablespoons chopped fresh cilantro

1 package (10 ounces) frozen corn kernels, thawed

1 ounce Cheddar cheese, grated

You can pipe the potatoes over the filling in a lattice pattern, using a plain or fluted wide tip or a large round tip.

Shepherd's pie, as the name suggests, is traditionally made with lamb or mutton (and sometimes with beef). This wonderfully warming rendition of the British favorite is quite different: It's a vegetarian dish, with a savory filling of potatoes and beans in tomato sauce, a layer of corn and a cheese-crowned mashed-potato crust. To dress the pie up a bit, you can pipe the potato topping through a pastry bag (see below), using a wide tip.

1 Preheat the oven to 375°.

2 Place the potatoes in a large saucepan and add water to cover. Cover the pan and bring to boil over high heat. Reduce the heat to medium, cover and simmer for 10 minutes, or until the potatoes are just tender.

3 Meanwhile, in a medium saucepan, combine the black beans, kidney beans, tomato sauce, onions, garlic and ¼ teaspoon each of the salt and black pepper. Bring to a boil over medium-high heat; reduce the heat to medium and simmer for 2 to 3 minutes, or just until heated through. Spread the bean mixture in an 11 x 7-inch baking dish and set aside.

4 When the potatoes are cooked, drain in a colander and return to the large pan. Add the milk, butter or margarine, cilantro and remaining ¼ teaspoon each salt and black pepper; mash with a potato masher until smooth.

5 Spread the corn over the bean mixture, then spread the mashed potatoes on top. Sprinkle with the Cheddar.

6 Bake the shepherd's pie for 20 minutes, or until the top is golden. Remove from the oven and place under the broiler for about 1 minute to brown the topping slightly.

Preparation time 15 minutes • **Total time** 50 minutes • **Per serving** 424 calories, 10.1 g. fat (21% of calories), 5.5 g. saturated fat, 24 mg. cholesterol, 716 mg. sodium, 11.8 g. dietary fiber, 175 mg. calcium, 5 mg. iron, 53 mg. vitamin C, 0.9 mg. beta-carotene • **Serves 4**

BAKED CHICKEN WITH ROOT VEGETABLES

¼ cup mixed fresh herbs (such as tarragon, basil, parsley and mint), minced

2 teaspoons grated lemon zest

2 garlic cloves, minced

1 broiler-fryer chicken (2¼ pounds), cut into 8 serving pieces

3 tablespoons fresh lemon juice

8 ounces small red potatoes, quartered

1 small fennel bulb, trimmed and quartered

2 medium turnips, peeled and cut into 1-inch pieces

3 medium carrots, cut into 2-inch pieces

3 shallots, quartered

½ cup defatted reduced-sodium chicken broth

½ teaspoon salt

¼ teaspoon freshly ground black pepper

Fresh thyme and tarragon sprigs, for garnish (optional)

Degreasing the pan juices is an important step in this recipe. The best tool for the job is a gravy separator, a clear cup with a spout that begins at the base (rather than the top). When you pour in fatty pan juices, soup or sauce, the fat rises to the top, allowing the defatted juices to be poured out through the spout.

1 Preheat the oven to 375°. Line a large roasting pan with foil.

2 In a small bowl, combine the herbs, lemon zest and garlic. Spread 2 tablespoons of this mixture under the skin of the chicken. Stir the lemon juice into the remaining herb mixture; set aside.

3 Arrange the chicken pieces on a rack at one end of the prepared roasting pan. Spread the potatoes, fennel, turnips, carrots and shallots on the rack at other end of the pan. Brush the chicken with half of the lemon-herb mixture. Drizzle the vegetables and chicken evenly with the broth, then sprinkle with the salt and black pepper.

4 Bake the chicken and vegetables for 15 minutes, then baste the chicken with the remaining lemon-herb mixture. Increase the oven temperature to 400° and continue to bake for another 25 minutes, or until the chicken is browned and cooked through.

5 Remove the pan from the oven and transfer the chicken and vegetables to a platter. Pour the juices remaining in the pan into a gravy separator. Pour the degreased pan juices over the chicken and vegetables. Garnish with thyme and tarragon sprigs, if desired. Remove the skin from the chicken before eating.

Preparation time 15 minutes • **Total time** 1 hour • **Per serving** 278 calories, 7 g. fat (23% of calories), 1.9 g. saturated fat, 81 mg. cholesterol, 537 mg. sodium, 4.4 g. dietary fiber, 80 mg. calcium, 3 mg. iron, 41 mg. vitamin C, 9.3 mg. beta-carotene • **Serves 4**

❧ ❧ ❧

KITCHEN TIP
If you don't have a gravy separator, use this trick for skimming the fat with a spoon: Pour the pan juices into a tall container, such as a glass measuring cup, rather than trying to skim them in the pan. This way, the fat will rise to the top in a deep layer, which is easier to remove.

TURKEY PRIMAVERA IN PARCHMENT

16 ounces fresh asparagus spears, trimmed and cut diagonally into ½-inch slices

2 medium carrots, cut into julienne strips

1 medium yellow bell pepper, cut into julienne strips

8 ounces fusilli or penne pasta

4 turkey cutlets (4 ounces each), pounded thin

1 tablespoon chopped fresh tarragon or thyme

1 teaspoon grated lemon zest

½ teaspoon salt

¼ teaspoon freshly ground black pepper

¼ cup fresh lemon juice

2 teaspoons reduced-sodium soy sauce

1 tablespoon olive oil

1 medium tomato, finely diced

2 tablespoons minced fresh chives

Lemon zest and fresh thyme sprigs, for garnish (optional)

Starting at the rounded end, fold over and crimp the edges of the parchment in a series of small pleats. When you reach the point of the heart, twist the "tail" to finish.

Few food-presentation techniques are as impressive as a *papillote,* or parchment-paper packet. (The name, close to the French word for butterfly, may derive from the fact that when the folded paper is cut into a heart shape, it looks like butterfly wings.) Rolls of kitchen parchment are sold in cookware shops.

1 Preheat the oven to 350°. Cut four 17 x 12-inch pieces of parchment paper or foil. If using parchment, fold each piece in half and cut into a half-heart shape.

2 Bring a large covered pot of water to a boil over high heat. Add the asparagus, carrots and bell peppers, and blanch for 2 minutes. Using a strainer or slotted spoon, transfer the vegetables to a large bowl; keep the water boiling.

3 Add the pasta to the boiling water, return to a boil and cook for 8 minutes (the pasta will not be fully cooked). Drain the pasta in a colander.

4 If using the parchment, unfold. Place one-fourth of the pasta on one side of each piece of parchment or at one end of each piece of foil. Place a turkey cutlet on top of the pasta and sprinkle with the tarragon or thyme, lemon zest, salt and black pepper. Spoon one-fourth of the vegetables on top of each, then sprinkle with the lemon juice, soy sauce and oil. Close the parchment or foil packets, sealing the edges with small folds.

5 Place the packets on a baking sheet and bake for 20 minutes, or until the parchment is puffed (the foil will not puff) and the turkey is cooked through (open one packet to check).

6 Place the packets on 4 plates and cut open. Top each with some diced tomato and minced chives, and garnish with lemon zest and thyme sprigs, if desired.

Preparation time 20 minutes • **Total time** 1 hour • **Per serving** 414 calories, 5.3 g. fat (12% of calories), 0.9 g. saturated fat, 70 mg. cholesterol, 451 mg. sodium, 3.9 g. dietary fiber, 57 mg. calcium, 5 mg. iron, 54 mg. vitamin C, 6.7 mg. beta-carotene • **Serves 4**

MACARONI 'N' CHEESE WITH CHICKEN

- 6 ounces macaroni, such as elbows
- 1 teaspoon olive oil
- 3 medium carrots, diced
- ½ cup chopped shallots
- 2 garlic cloves, minced
- 1 teaspoon chopped fresh thyme or ½ teaspoon dried thyme
- ½ teaspoon salt
- ¼ teaspoon freshly ground black pepper
- ⅛ teaspoon ground red pepper
- 1 tablespoon cornstarch
- 1½ cups 1% low-fat milk
- 2 ounces Cheddar cheese, shredded
- 2 tablespoons grated Romano cheese
- 1 tablespoon Dijon mustard
- 4 ounces skinless smoked chicken breast, diced
- 1 package (10 ounces) frozen chopped spinach, thawed and squeezed dry
- ½ cup unseasoned dry breadcrumbs
- 2 tablespoons chopped Italian parsley

Dear as your childhood memories may be of bright orange macaroni and cheese, now you'd probably prefer one of these individual gratins, filled with macaroni, chunks of smoked chicken and spinach in a sophisticated Cheddar-Romano sauce.

1 Preheat the oven to 375°. Spray four 1½-cup gratin dishes or an 11 x 7-inch baking dish with no-stick spray.

2 Bring a large covered pot of water to a boil over high heat. Add the macaroni to the boiling water, return to a boil and cook for 6 to 7 minutes, or according to package directions until al dente. Drain in a colander, rinse briefly under cold running water and drain again.

3 While the pasta is cooking, in a large saucepan, warm the oil over medium-high heat. Add the carrots, shallots and garlic, and sauté for 2 to 3 minutes, or until the vegetables are softened. Stir in the thyme, salt, black pepper and ground red pepper, and cook, stirring, for 30 seconds, or until fragrant.

4 In a small bowl, whisk the cornstarch with ½ cup of the milk. Add the cornstarch mixture to the saucepan along with the remaining 1 cup milk; increase the heat to high and bring to a boil, stirring constantly. Reduce the heat to medium and simmer for 1 minute.

5 Whisk in the Cheddar, Romano and mustard until smooth. Remove the pan from the heat and add the smoked chicken, spinach and drained macaroni; stir gently to combine. Spoon the mixture into the prepared gratin dishes or baking dish.

6 In a small bowl, combine the breadcrumbs and parsley. Sprinkle the breadcrumb mixture over the top of the macaroni. Bake for 20 to 25 minutes, or until hot and bubbly.

Preparation time 20 minutes • **Total time** 1 hour • **Per serving** 437 calories, 11.2 g. fat (23% of calories), 4.4 g. saturated fat, 33 mg. cholesterol, 987 mg. sodium, 5.1 g. dietary fiber, 393 mg. calcium, 5 mg. iron, 27 mg. vitamin C, 12.7 mg. beta-carotene • **Serves 4**

❧　❧　❧

Stir-Fries & Other Skillet Meals

❧ ❧ ❧

POPULAR PAN DINNERS INSPIRED BY

THE WORLD'S GREAT CUISINES

DOUBLE ORANGE BEEF WITH VEGETABLES

2¼ cups plus ⅓ cup water

2 cups quick-cooking brown rice

⅓ cup fresh orange juice

2 tablespoons orange marmalade

2 tablespoons reduced-sodium
soy sauce

1½ teaspoons cornstarch

¼ teaspoon crushed red pepper
flakes

12 ounces lean, trimmed boneless
beef sirloin or top round steak,
thinly sliced

½ pound fresh asparagus spears,
trimmed and diagonally sliced
into 1-inch pieces

2 medium carrots, thinly sliced on
the diagonal

2 teaspoons vegetable oil

1 medium red bell pepper, cut
into thin strips

4 ounces shiitake or white
mushrooms, sliced

3 large scallions, thinly sliced on
the diagonal

2 garlic cloves, minced

½ teaspoon grated fresh ginger

Rice turns this stir-fry into a well-rounded meal, and quick-cooking brown rice, used here, is a great time-saver. Alternatively, you could cook regular brown rice the night before you plan to serve this dish, then reheat it while you stir-fry the vegetables and beef. Add a little water or broth to the rice before reheating in a covered pot over gentle heat.

1 In a medium saucepan, bring 2¼ cups of the water to a boil over high heat. Stir in the rice and reduce the heat to medium-low; cover and simmer for 10 minutes, or until the rice is tender and the liquid is absorbed. Remove the pan from the heat and set aside.

2 While the rice is cooking, in a medium bowl, combine the orange juice, marmalade, soy sauce, cornstarch and red pepper flakes, stirring until smooth. Stir in the beef and let stand while you prepare the vegetables.

3 In a large no-stick skillet, bring the remaining ⅓ cup of water to a boil over medium-high heat. Add the asparagus and carrots, cover and cook for 3 minutes, or until the vegetables are just tender. Drain the vegetables in a colander and transfer to a medium bowl. Wipe the skillet dry.

4 In the dry skillet, warm 1 teaspoon of the oil over medium-high heat. Add the bell peppers and mushrooms, and stir-fry for 2 minutes, or until the vegtables are tender. Add the scallions, garlic and ginger, and stir-fry for 30 seconds, or until fragrant. Transfer to the bowl with the other vegetables.

5 Add the remaining 1 teaspoon oil to the skillet. Add the beef and the marinade, and stir-fry for 3 to 4 minutes, or until the beef is cooked through. Add the vegetables and stir-fry for 1 minute, or until the vegetables are heated through. Fluff the rice with a fork and serve with the beef and vegetables.

Preparation time 25 minutes • **Total time** 35 minutes • **Per serving** 399 calories, 8.4 g. fat (18% of calories), 1.7 g. saturated fat, 52 mg. cholesterol, 395 mg. sodium, 4.8 g. dietary fiber, 51 mg. calcium, 4 mg. iron, 70 mg. vitamin C, 7.1 mg. beta-carotene • **Serves 4**

❧ ❧ ❧

Preceding pages: Mediterranean-Style Tuna and Pasta (recipe on page 80)

TURKEY-VEGETABLE HASH

- 2 pounds small red potatoes, quartered

- ½ teaspoon salt

- 1 cup diced carrots

- 1 tablespoon plus 1 teaspoon olive oil

- 1 medium green bell pepper, diced

- 1 medium onion, diced

- 2 garlic cloves, minced

- ½ cup defatted reduced-sodium chicken broth

- ¾ teaspoon dried thyme or 1 tablespoon fresh, chopped thyme

- ½ teaspoon dried sage or 1 tablespoon fresh sage

- ½ teaspoon freshly ground black pepper

- 12 ounces skinless roast turkey breast (in one piece), cut into ½-inch cubes

- ¼ cup chopped Italian parsley

Think of the best hash-browns you ever ate for breakfast. Now imagine those same crisp potatoes amplified with carrots, peppers and chunks of turkey and glorified with garlic and herbs. You'd have to agree it's a wonderfully homey idea for a simple supper.

1 Preheat the broiler. Place the potatoes in a medium saucepan with water to cover and ¼ teaspoon of the salt; cover the pan and bring to a boil over high heat. Boil for 2 minutes; add the carrots and boil for 4 minutes longer, or until tender. Drain the vegetables in a colander.

2 While the potatoes and carrots are cooking, in a large flameproof skillet, warm the oil over medium-high heat. Add the bell peppers, onions and garlic, and sauté for 2 to 3 minutes, or until tender.

3 Stir in the potatoes and carrots, the broth, thyme, sage, black pepper and remaining ¼ teaspoon salt. Cook, stirring frequently, for 7 minutes, or until the hash starts to brown. Reduce the heat to medium-low, stir in the turkey and parsley, and cook for 2 minutes.

4 Place the skillet under the broiler and broil the hash 4 to 5 inches from the heat for 2 minutes, or until the top is browned and crisp.

Preparation time 25 minutes • **Total time** 50 minutes • **Per serving** 378 calories, 5.8 g. fat (14% of calories), 0.9 g. saturated fat, 71 mg. cholesterol, 429 mg. sodium, 5.9 g. dietary fiber, 45 mg. calcium, 4 mg. iron, 61 mg. vitamin C, 4.8 mg. beta-carotene • **Serves 4**

Italian parsley has flat, deeply toothed leaves. It's considered superior in flavor to curly and is preferable for seasoning.

Curly parsley, with its frilled leaves, is a fine addition to salads and makes a pretty garnish for many main dishes.

GREEK SKILLET DINNER IN A PITA

1 tablespoon plus 1 teaspoon
olive oil

1 pound eggplant, cut into ¾-inch
cubes

¼ cup defatted reduced-sodium
chicken broth

12 ounces lean, well-trimmed
boneless leg of lamb or beef top
round, cut into ½-inch chunks

1 medium onion, chopped

2 celery stalks, diced

3 garlic cloves, minced

2 teaspoons ground cumin

½ teaspoon dried oregano

¼ teaspoon dried mint or
2 tablespoons fresh mint

¼ teaspoon salt

¼ teaspoon freshly ground black
pepper

1 can (14½ ounces) diced
tomatoes with juice

1 can (10 ounces) chick-peas,
rinsed and drained

4 pita breads (6-inch diameter),
halved

½ cup plain nonfat yogurt

4 cups shredded Romaine lettuce

1 cup peeled, sliced cucumbers

2 plum tomatoes, thinly sliced

Chopped fresh mint, for garnish
(optional)

Long before you could buy skillet-dinner mixes in a box, cooks were stirring up ground meat, vegetables and favorite seasonings to feed the family economically and well. Resembling an exotic street snack more than a traditional skillet dinner, this delicious lamb-and-eggplant mixture is served in pitas.

1 In a large, heavy skillet, warm 2 teaspoons of the oil over medium-high heat. Add the eggplant and sauté for 2 to 3 minutes, or until browned. Stir in the broth and bring to a boil; reduce the heat to medium and cook for about 4 minutes, or until the eggplant is tender and the liquid is absorbed. Transfer the eggplant to a large plate.

2 Meanwhile, process the lamb or beef in a food processor until coarsely ground.

3 In the large skillet, warm the remaining 2 teaspoons oil over medium-high heat. Add the onions, celery and garlic, and sauté for 2 to 3 minutes, or until the onions are tender. Crumble in the ground meat and cook, stirring, for 3 minutes, or until the meat is no longer pink. Stir in the cumin, oregano, mint, salt and black pepper; cook, stirring constantly, for 30 seconds.

4 Add the tomatoes and their juice, and bring to a boil. Stir in the chick-peas and the reserved eggplant. Reduce the heat to low and simmer, stirring occasionally, for 5 to 7 minutes to blend the flavors.

5 Spoon one-fourth of the lamb mixture into each pita. Serve with the yogurt, lettuce, cucumbers and tomatoes, and garnish with chopped fresh mint, if desired.

Preparation time 25 minutes • **Total time** 40 minutes • **Per serving** 475 calories, 11.1 g. fat (21% of calories), 2.2 g. saturated fat, 55 mg. cholesterol, 851 mg. sodium, 7.9 g. dietary fiber, 257 mg. calcium, 7 mg. iron, 45 mg. vitamin C, 1.5 mg. beta-carotene • **Serves 4**

❧ ❧ ❧

FOR A CHANGE
Instead of spooning the lamb mixture into pitas, serve it over hot pasta, with a sprinkling of feta cheese.

MARKET AND PANTRY
With eggplants, think "handsome is as handsome does." The shiniest, plumpest, purplest and smoothest are those to buy.

SPICY VEGETABLE FRITTATA

2 teaspoons olive oil

1 pound small red potatoes, diced

1 cup diced red bell pepper

1 small onion, diced

¼ cup defatted reduced-sodium chicken broth

1 cup diced zucchini

½ cup sliced scallions

2 garlic cloves, minced

¾ teaspoon dried thyme

½ teaspoon dried oregano

½ teaspoon salt

¼ teaspoon freshly ground black pepper

⅛ teaspoon ground red pepper

3 large whole eggs

6 large egg whites

¼ cup 1% low-fat milk

1 ounce Parmesan cheese, coarsely grated

1 cup seeded, diced tomato

2 tablespoons chopped Italian parsley

French folded omelets are delicious to eat but tricky to make. It is much easier to put together an Italian frittata, in which the ingredients that would serve as the filling for a folded omelet are simply mixed with the beaten eggs. This frittata uses just three whole eggs for four servings (six additional egg whites add a fluffy lightness but contribute no fat or cholesterol). It's packed with potatoes, peppers and onions, and topped with fresh tomatoes for an instant "relish."

1 In a large no-stick skillet, warm the oil over medium-high heat. Add the potatoes, bell peppers and onions, and cook for 2 minutes, or until the vegetables begin to brown. Add the broth and cook, stirring occasionally, for about 5 minutes, or until the potatoes begin to soften. Stir in the zucchini, scallions, garlic, thyme, oregano, salt, black pepper and ground red pepper, and cook for 4 minutes, or until the vegetables are tender and golden.

2 Meanwhile, in a medium bowl, whisk together the whole eggs, egg whites, milk and Parmesan.

3 Pour the egg mixture all at once over the vegetables and reduce the heat to medium-low. Stir to combine the eggs and vegetables, then cook, without stirring, for 10 minutes, or until the mixture begins to set.

4 Cover the skillet and cook for 2 minutes longer, or until the eggs are set on top. Slide the frittata onto a serving plate and sprinkle with the tomatoes and parsley.

Preparation time 25 minutes • **Total time** 40 minutes • **Per serving** 268 calories, 8.6 g. fat (28% of calories), 2.8 g. saturated fat, 165 mg. cholesterol, 583 mg. sodium, 3.9 g. dietary fiber, 164 mg. calcium, 3 mg. iron, 83 mg. vitamin C, 1.4 mg. beta-carotene • **Serves 4**

KITCHEN TIP
Rather than separating an egg by dropping the yolk from one half shell to the other (you're all too likely to break a yolk and waste an egg), buy an inexpensive egg separator. This tool looks like a big spoon with a slotted bowl; when you break an egg into the center, the yolk is held in the inner bowl while the white flows out through the slots on the sides.

MEDITERRANEAN-STYLE TUNA AND PASTA

1 pint (8 ounces) cherry
tomatoes, stemmed and halved

2 tablespoons rinsed and drained
capers

2 tablespoons chopped fresh dill

2 garlic cloves, minced

2 teaspoons grated lemon zest

2 teaspoons olive oil

½ teaspoon salt

½ teaspoon freshly ground black
pepper

8 ounces penne pasta

1½ pounds spinach, trimmed and
chopped

8 ounces tuna steak, cut into
1-inch cubes

2 ounces feta cheese, crumbled

This meal is almost like a salad in a skillet—light and fresh and full of vegetables. In fact, you needn't rush to the table with the dish, as it would be delicious served warm, in the manner of many stylish dinner salads. The fresh tuna, tomatoes, herbs, garlic, olive oil and capers reflect its Mediterranean roots.

1 Bring a large covered pot of water to a boil over high heat.

2 In a large bowl, combine the cherry tomatoes, capers, dill, garlic, lemon zest, olive oil and ¼ teaspoon each of the salt and black pepper.

3 Add the penne to the boiling water, return to a boil and cook for 8 to 10 minutes, or according to package directions until al dente. During the last 1 minute of cooking, add the spinach. Drain the pasta and spinach together in a colander.

4 Add the pasta and spinach to the tomato mixture, and toss gently to combine.

5 Spray a large no-stick skillet with no-stick spray. Add the tuna and cook over medium-high heat for 3 to 5 minutes, or just until browned. Add the remaining ¼ teaspoon each salt and black pepper, and toss with the tuna.

6 Add the pasta and spinach mixture to the tuna in the skillet, then stir in the feta cheese; toss well. Cook for 1 minute to heat through.

Preparation time 15 minutes • **Total time** 30 minutes • **Per serving** 395 calories, 9.8 g. fat (22% of calories), 3.3 g. saturated fat, 34 mg. cholesterol, 671 mg. sodium, 5.4 g. dietary fiber, 218 mg. calcium, 7 mg. iron, 47 mg. vitamin C, 5.9 mg. beta-carotene • **Serves 4**

The tiny, tight buds of "nonpareil" capers (on the left) are considered superior to the larger capers on the right. Nonpareils are slightly more expensive.

FOR A CHANGE
Scallops are a delicious variation on this recipe. Use 8 ounces of sea scallops; halve any that are very large. Sauté the scallops for 4 to 5 minutes, or until opaque. You can vary the seasonings, too: Fresh dill is wonderful with fish and shellfish, but you could try other fresh herbs, such as tarragon or oregano, when available.

ON THE MENU
Serve lime sorbet with fresh or frozen raspberries for a pretty, refreshing finale.

CHICKEN SUCCOTASH

2 teaspoons olive oil

12 ounces skinless, boneless chicken breast halves, cut into ½-inch chunks

½ teaspoon dried thyme

½ teaspoon salt

¼ teaspoon freshly ground black pepper

Pinch of ground nutmeg

Pinch of ground red pepper

1 medium red bell pepper, diced

2 celery stalks, finely diced

½ cup chopped shallots or onion

6 ounces ditalini or other small pasta

1 package (10 ounces) frozen baby lima beans

1 cup defatted reduced-sodium chicken broth

1 cup frozen corn kernels

1 tablespoon cornstarch

¾ cup 1% low-fat milk

2 tablespoons chopped Italian parsley

Ascending from side-dish to main-dish status, this succotash takes on some new components; indeed, the Native Americans who introduced this sturdy fare to the Pilgrims would probably not recognize their creation. In addition to the traditional lima beans and corn, there are chicken chunks, pasta, peppers, shallots and celery in this tasty rendition of a longtime American favorite.

1 Bring a large covered pot of water to a boil over high heat.

2 In a large no-stick skillet, warm the oil over medium-high heat. Add the chicken, thyme, salt, black pepper, nutmeg and ground red pepper, and sauté for 3 minutes, or until the chicken turns golden. Stir in the bell peppers, celery and shallots or onions, and sauté for 3 minutes, or until the vegetables begin to soften.

3 Add the pasta to the boiling water, return to a boil and cook for 10 to 12 minutes, or according to package directions until al dente. Drain in a colander and return to the pot to keep warm.

4 While the pasta is cooking, add the lima beans and broth to the skillet and bring to a boil. Reduce the heat to medium-low and simmer for 10 minutes. Stir in the corn and simmer for 1 minute longer, or until heated through.

5 In a cup, whisk the cornstarch with ¼ cup of the milk. Stir the cornstarch mixture into the chicken mixture, then stir in the remaining ½ cup milk. Simmer for 1 minute, or until slightly thickened. Add the chicken to the pasta and toss to combine. Divide the succotash among 4 plates and sprinkle each serving with some chopped parsley.

Preparation time 20 minutes • **Total time** 40 minutes • **Per serving** 456 calories, 5.2 g. fat (10% of calories), 1.1 g. saturated fat, 51 mg. cholesterol, 575 mg. sodium, 5.9 g. dietary fiber, 125 mg. calcium, 5 mg. iron, 51 mg. vitamin C, 0.9 mg. beta-carotene • **Serves 4**

❧ ❧ ❧

FOOD FACT
Ditalini are small pasta cuts shaped like open-ended thimbles (ditalini means "thimbles"). The pasta is close in size to the corn kernels and lima beans, giving the dish a pleasing texture. The small shell pasta called conchigliette, or even small elbow macaroni, could also be used.

SHRIMP WITH LEMON AND ALMONDS

¼ cup fresh lemon juice

2 tablespoons rice wine vinegar

1 tablespoon plus 1 teaspoon sugar

1 teaspoon grated lemon zest

⅛ teaspoon crushed red pepper flakes

1 tablespoon plus 1 teaspoon reduced-sodium soy sauce

1 tablespoon dry sherry

2 teaspoons cornstarch

12 ounces medium shrimp, peeled and deveined, with tails attached

¼ cup blanched slivered almonds

1 tablespoon plus 1 teaspoon vegetable oil

8 ounces sugar snap peas or snow peas, trimmed

1 medium red bell pepper, diced

1 medium yellow bell pepper, diced

1 small onion, diced

2 garlic cloves, minced

2 tablespoons water

½ cup sliced water chestnuts

2 tablespoons chopped Italian parsley

6 ounces fresh cappellini pasta

Here's an eclectic meal worthy of today's hot young chefs—who often label such dishes "fusion cuisine." While many of the ingredients (soy sauce, rice wine vinegar and water chestnuts) and techniques ("velvet-coating" the shrimp with a cornstarch mixture and stir-frying) are Asian, the stir-fried shrimp and vegetables are served over cappellini pasta in classic Italian style.

1 Bring a large covered pot of water to a boil over high heat. Meanwhile, in a small bowl, whisk together the lemon juice, vinegar, sugar, lemon zest and red pepper flakes until blended; set aside.

2 In a medium bowl, whisk together the soy sauce, sherry and cornstarch until smooth. Add the shrimp and toss to coat. Refrigerate for 15 minutes.

3 Meanwhile, in a large skillet over medium-high heat, toast the almonds, tossing frequently, for 2 to 3 minutes, or until golden. Transfer to a small bowl.

4 In the large skillet, warm 2 teaspoons of the oil over medium-high heat until very hot but not smoking. Add the peas, peppers, onions and garlic, and stir-fry for 1 minute. Add the water, cover and cook for 2 minutes, or until the vegetables are just tender. Transfer to a plate.

5 In the large skillet, warm the remaining 2 teaspoons oil over medium-high heat. Add the shrimp and the marinade, and stir-fry for 5 to 6 minutes, or just until the shrimp turn pink and opaque. Stir in the lemon-juice mixture, reduce the heat to medium and simmer for 1 minute. Stir in the vegetables, water chestnuts and parsley. Sprinkle with the toasted almonds and remove the pan from the heat.

6 Add the cappellini to the boiling water; return to a boil and cook for 30 to 45 seconds, or until the pasta is al dente. Drain in a colander. Divide the pasta among 4 plates and top with the shrimp mixture.

Preparation time 25 minutes • **Total time** 30 minutes • **Per serving** 391 calories, 11.3 g. fat (26% of calories), 1.4 g. saturated fat, 136 mg. cholesterol, 378 mg. sodium, 4.3 g. dietary fiber, 121 mg. calcium, 4 mg. iron, 68 mg. vitamin C, 0.8 mg. beta-carotene • **Serves 4**

SKILLET CASSOULET

1 teaspoon olive oil

2 ounces reduced-fat turkey
kielbasa sausage, halved and
sliced ½-inch thick

1 medium onion, chopped

2 celery stalks, diced

2 medium carrots, diced

8 ounces skinless, boneless
chicken thighs, cut into 1-inch
chunks

2 garlic cloves, minced

1 bay leaf, preferably imported

½ teaspoon dried rosemary or
1 tablespoon fresh rosemary

½ teaspoon dried thyme or
1 tablespoon fresh thyme

¼ teaspoon freshly ground black
pepper

1 can (14½ ounces) stewed
tomatoes with juice

¼ cup white wine

2 cans (19 ounces each)
cannellini beans, rinsed and
drained

1 cup fresh breadcrumbs

¼ cup chopped Italian parsley

If you love the French country casserole called cassoulet—but don't have time to soak the dried beans, roast the duck, poach the sausage, blanch the salt pork, brown the lamb and bake the casserole (whew!)—this recipe will please you. And you'll love the big cuts in fat and calories, thanks to the use of turkey kielbasa and chicken.

1 In a large flameproof skillet, warm the oil over medium-high heat. Add the sausage, onions, celery and carrots; cover and cook, stirring occasionally, for 5 minutes, or until the vegetables are tender.

2 Add the chicken to the skillet and cook, turning occasionally, for 3 to 5 minutes, or until browned on all sides. Stir in the garlic, bay leaf, rosemary, thyme and black pepper, and cook for 30 seconds, or until fragrant. Add the tomatoes and their juice, then add the wine. Reduce the heat to medium-low and simmer, covered, for 10 minutes. Stir in the beans and simmer, covered, for 5 minutes longer. While the cassoulet is cooking, preheat the broiler.

3 In a small bowl, combine the breadcrumbs and parsley. Sprinkle the top of the cassoulet with the breadcrumb mixture. Broil for 2 minutes, or until the topping is golden.

Preparation time 25 minutes • **Total time** 40 minutes • **Per serving** 396 calories, 6.8 g. fat (16% of calories), 1.4 g. saturated fat, 57 mg. cholesterol, 861 mg. sodium, 15.7 g. dietary fiber, 7 mg. calcium, 6 mg. iron, 30 mg. vitamin C, 6.6 mg. beta-carotene • **Serves 4**

❧ ❧ ❧

To make your own breadcrumbs, trim the crusts from an unsliced loaf of bread.

Then grate the crustless bread on the large holes of a hand grater.

Or, place large chunks of the bread in a food processor and pulse to make crumbs.

HOISIN PORK AND VEGETABLES

- 2 tablespoons hoisin sauce
- 2 tablespoons dry sherry
- 2 tablespoons reduced-sodium soy sauce
- 1 tablespoon honey
- 1½ teaspoons cornstarch
- ½ teaspoon dark sesame oil
- ¼ teaspoon crushed red pepper flakes
- 8 ounces lean, boneless pork loin, cut into ¼-inch-wide strips
- 8 ounces whole-wheat spaghettini
- ⅔ cup water
- 6 cups broccoli florets or 8 cups trimmed, cut-up broccoli rabe (2-inch lengths)
- 2 medium carrots, sliced
- 3 teaspoons vegetable oil
- 2 cups thinly sliced red cabbage
- 1 medium yellow bell pepper, sliced
- ½ small red onion, sliced
- 2 garlic cloves, minced

Hoisin sauce, which gives this pork stir-fry savory richness, is a Chinese staple that's sold in most American supermarkets. If you like to create your own stir-fried dishes, there should be a bottle of hoisin sauce in your refrigerator. Made from soybeans, vinegar, garlic, chilies and spices, this sauce can season meat, poultry and shellfish (you can use it in cooking, or as a table condiment). If you buy hoisin sauce in a can, transfer it to a glass jar before you store it.

1 In a medium bowl, combine the hoisin sauce, sherry, soy sauce, honey, cornstarch, sesame oil and red pepper flakes. Stir in the pork and let marinate while you prepare the pasta and vegetables.

2 While the pork is marinating, bring a large covered pot of water to a boil over high heat. Add the spaghettini, return to a boil and cook for 10 to 12 minutes, or according to package directions until al dente. Drain in a colander.

3 While the spaghettini is cooking, in a large no-stick skillet, bring the ⅔ cup of water to a boil over high heat. Add the broccoli florets or broccoli rabe and the carrots, cover and cook for 2 minutes, or until the vegetables are just tender. Drain the vegetables in a colander and transfer to a medium bowl. Wipe the skillet dry.

4 In the dry skillet, warm 1 teaspoon of the oil over medium-high heat. Add the cabbage, bell peppers and onions, and stir-fry for 2 to 3 minutes, or until tender. Add the garlic and stir-fry for 30 seconds, or until fragrant. Transfer to the bowl with the other vegetables.

5 In the skillet, warm the remaining 2 teaspoons oil over medium-high heat. Add the pork and the marinade, and stir-fry for 2 to 3 minutes, or until the pork is cooked through. Add the vegetables and stir-fry for 1 to 2 minutes, or until heated through. Serve over the spaghettini.

Preparation time 25 minutes • **Total time** 35 minutes • **Per serving** 468 calories, 8.8 g. fat (16% of calories), 1.8 g. saturated fat, 33 mg. cholesterol, 557 mg. sodium, 15.8 g. dietary fiber, 155 mg. calcium, 5 mg. iron, 182 mg. vitamin C, 8 mg. beta-carotene • **Serves 4**

SEAFOOD JAMBALAYA

- 1 tablespoon olive oil
- 3 ounces baked ham, diced
- 1 medium green bell pepper, diced
- 1 medium onion, chopped
- 2 celery stalks, chopped
- 3 garlic cloves, minced
- 1 cup long-grain white rice
- 1 bay leaf, preferably imported
- ½ teaspoon dried oregano
- ½ teaspoon dried thyme
- ½ teaspoon freshly ground black pepper
- ¼ teaspoon salt
- ⅛ teaspoon ground red pepper
- 1½ cups defatted reduced-sodium chicken broth
- 1½ cups water
- 8 ounces sea scallops, tough muscle removed
- 8 ounces medium shrimp, peeled and deveined, with tails attached
- 1 cup diced ripe tomatoes
- ¼ cup chopped Italian parsley

Not many foods have found their way into the lyrics of American popular songs: Jambalaya (and its Cajun companions, crawfish pie and filé gumbo) has that rare distinction. One of the defining dishes of Louisiana cuisine, jambalaya is delightfully variable, subject to the whims of the person cooking it (although the rice, onions, celery and bell peppers are unvarying ingredients). The shrimp-scallop-and-ham jambalaya here is just one interpretation of a dish that is frequently made with sausage, crayfish or oysters.

1 In a large no-stick skillet, warm the oil over medium-high heat. Add the ham, bell peppers, onions, celery and garlic, and sauté for 4 to 5 minutes, or until the vegetables are softened.

2 Stir in the rice, bay leaf, oregano, thyme, black pepper, salt and ground red pepper, and sauté for 1 minute. Add the broth and water, and bring to a boil. Reduce the heat to medium-low, cover and simmer for 15 minutes, or until the rice is just tender.

3 Stir in the scallops, shrimp and tomatoes; cover and simmer for 5 minutes, or until the seafood turns opaque. Just before serving, sprinkle the jambalaya with the chopped parsley.

Preparation time 25 minutes • **Total time** 35 minutes • **Per serving** 383 calories, 7.2 g. fat (17% of calories), 1.5 g. saturated fat, 101 mg. cholesterol, 883 mg. sodium, 2.6 g. dietary fiber, 92 mg. calcium, 5 mg. iron, 38 mg. vitamin C, 0.4 mg. beta-carotene • **Serves 4**

To chop an onion, first cut off the tip and peel the onion. Make a series of parallel cuts toward (but not through) the root end.

Holding the partially sliced onion together, make a second, perpendicular series of cuts, without cutting all the way through.

Still holding the onion together, turn it on its side and cut crosswise: The onion will fall into tiny dice.

STIR-FRY CHICKEN CURRY WITH SPINACH

1¼ cups plus 2 tablespoons water

1 cup instant couscous

2 garlic cloves, minced

1 tablespoon curry powder

1 teaspoon grated fresh ginger

1 teaspoon tomato paste

1 teaspoon ground cumin

¼ teaspoon salt

¼ teaspoon freshly ground black pepper

Pinch of ground cloves

1½ teaspoons vegetable oil

1 medium onion, finely chopped

12 ounces skinless, boneless chicken thighs, cut into 1½-inch chunks

12 ounces sweet potatoes, peeled and cut into ½-inch dice

1 cup defatted reduced-sodium chicken broth

1 cup diced Golden Delicious apple

½ cup frozen peas

4 ounces spinach, trimmed and coarsely chopped

¼ cup chopped fresh cilantro

Curry is normally a slow-simmered production, as it takes at least an hour for cubes of lamb or beef to cook to the point of melting tenderness. An obvious shortcut for curry-lovers who are pressed for time is to use chicken instead of red meat. After the chicken chunks are stir-fried, they simmer—along with diced sweet potatoes—for just 15 minutes or so in a spicy sauce. In another noteworthy departure from tradition, the curry is served over couscous rather than rice.

1 In a small saucepan, bring 1¼ cups of the water to a boil over high heat. Add the couscous, cover and remove from the heat. Let stand while you prepare the chicken and vegetables.

2 In a small bowl, combine the remaining 2 tablespoons of water, the garlic, curry powder, ginger, tomato paste, cumin, salt, black pepper and cloves, and whisk until smooth; set aside.

3 In a large no-stick skillet, warm the oil over medium-high heat until very hot but not smoking. Add the onions and stir-fry for 2 to 3 minutes, or until golden. Add the chicken and stir-fry for 4 minutes, or until browned. Stir in the garlic and reserved spice mixture, and stir-fry for about 1 minute, or until fragrant.

4 Add the potatoes and broth. Reduce the heat to medium-low, cover and simmer, stirring occasionally, for 10 to 15 minutes, or until the chicken is cooked through and the potatoes are tender. Stir in the apples and peas, cover and simmer for 3 minutes. Stir in the spinach and cook, uncovered, for 1 minute, or until the spinach is wilted.

5 Fluff the couscous with a fork and divide among 4 plates. Top the couscous with the curry, then sprinkle with the cilantro.

Preparation time 35 minutes • **Total time** 45 minutes • **Per serving** 420 calories, 6.2 g. fat (13% of calories), 1.2 g. saturated fat, 71 mg. cholesterol, 433 mg. sodium, 6.5 g. dietary fiber, 86 mg. calcium, 4 mg. iron, 31 mg. vitamin C, 8.4 mg. beta-carotene • **Serves 4**

❧ ❧ ❧

FIVE-SPICE CHICKEN WITH VEGETABLES

2 tablespoons reduced-sodium soy sauce

2 garlic cloves, minced

1½ teaspoons five-spice powder

1 teaspoon grated fresh ginger

1 teaspoon dark sesame oil

¼ teaspoon freshly ground black pepper

12 ounces thin-sliced chicken cutlets

⅓ cup defatted reduced-sodium chicken broth

1 tablespoon dry sherry

2 teaspoons cornstarch

⅛ teaspoon crushed red pepper flakes

3 teaspoons vegetable oil

6 ounces orzo pasta

½ pound green beans, trimmed

4 medium carrots, cut into julienne strips

3 cups small cauliflower florets

½ small red onion, thinly sliced

2 tablespoons water

Sliced scallion greens for garnish (optional)

Like pumpkin-pie spice or *fines herbes*, Chinese five-spice powder is a convenient ready-made seasoning blend. It's usually composed of ground anise or fennel seed, star anise, cloves, cinnamon and Szechuan peppercorns. You can find this unique spice blend at Asian markets, and many supermarkets stock it, too.

1 In a medium bowl, combine 2 teaspoons of the soy sauce, the garlic, five-spice powder, ginger, sesame oil and black pepper. Add the chicken and turn to coat. Refrigerate for 15 minutes.

2 Meanwhile, bring a large covered pot of water to a boil over high heat. In a small bowl, whisk together the broth, sherry, cornstarch, red pepper flakes and remaining 1 tablespoon plus 1 teaspoon soy sauce until smooth; set aside.

3 In a large no-stick skillet, warm 1½ teaspoons of the oil over medium-high heat until hot but not smoking. Add the chicken cutlets and cook, turning once, for 4 minutes, or until golden and cooked through. Transfer the chicken to a cutting board and cut into ¼-inch-wide strips.

4 Add the orzo to the boiling water, return to a boil and cook for 8 minutes, or according to package directions until al dente.

5 While the orzo is cooking, in the large skillet, warm the remaining 1½ teaspoons oil over medium-high heat until very hot but not smoking. Add the beans, carrots, cauliflower and onions, and cook, stirring, for 1 minute. Add the water, cover and cook for 2 minutes, or until the vegetables are just tender. Stir in the reserved chicken-broth mixture; reduce the heat to medium-low and simmer for 1 minute. Add the chicken and cook for 30 seconds longer.

6 Drain the orzo and divide it among 4 plates. Top with the chicken and vegetables, and garnish with sliced scallion greens, if desired.

Preparation time 25 minutes • **Total time** 35 minutes • **Per serving** 384 calories, 6.8 g. fat (16% of calories), 1 g. saturated fat, 49 mg. cholesterol, 454 mg. sodium, 6.5 g. dietary fiber, 86 mg. calcium, 4 mg. iron, 72 mg. vitamin C, 12.4 mg. beta-carotene • **Serves 4**

LONE STAR TURKEY TAMALE PIE

8 ounces skinless, boneless turkey cutlets, cut into chunks

1 teaspoon dried oregano

½ teaspoon fennel seeds

¼ teaspoon freshly ground black pepper

2 teaspoons olive oil

1 medium onion, chopped

3 garlic cloves, minced

2 medium zucchini, diced

2 tablespoons chili powder

1 teaspoon ground cumin

½ teaspoon ground coriander

¼ cup defatted reduced-sodium chicken broth

1 can (16 ounces) whole tomatoes in purée, coarsely chopped, with purée reserved

1 can (15 ounces) pinto beans, rinsed and drained

1 package (10 ounces) frozen corn kernels

1 can (4 ounces) chopped mild green chilies, rinsed and drained

3 cups water

¼ teaspoon salt

1 cup yellow cornmeal

2 ounces reduced-fat Cheddar cheese, shredded

Authentic Mexican tamales are not easy to prepare. They're made by enclosing a filling (such as chili-spiced chopped meat) in cornmeal dough and then in a cornhusk, securing the packets with a strip of cornhusk and then steaming the tamales. If you don't have this traditional technique down pat, try tamale pie, a favorite Southwestern casserole that captures the flavors without the work. You can see how much simpler it is to prepare the filling in a skillet, top it with a Cheddar-flavored cornmeal mixture and bake it in the oven.

1 Preheat the oven to 425°.

2 Process the turkey in a food processor until finely ground. Add the oregano, fennel seeds and black pepper, and pulse briefly.

3 In a large ovenproof skillet, warm the oil over medium-high heat. Add the onions and garlic, and sauté for 3 minutes, or until the onions are golden. Add the zucchini and sauté for 2 minutes. Stir in the turkey mixture, the chili powder, cumin and coriander, and cook, stirring constantly, for 1 minute. Add the broth and cook, stirring to break up any clumps of turkey, for 2 to 3 minutes, or until the turkey turns white.

4 Stir in the tomatoes and their purée, the beans, corn and chilies, and bring to a boil. Reduce the heat to medium-low and simmer for 5 minutes to blend the flavors; remove the pan from the heat.

5 Meanwhile, in a large saucepan, bring the water and salt to a boil over high heat. Gradually whisk in the cornmeal. Reduce the heat to low and cook, whisking frequently, for 5 minutes. Add the Cheddar and stir until melted.

6 Spoon the cornmeal mixture over the turkey mixture in the skillet. Bake for 15 minutes, or until the turkey mixture is bubbly and the cornmeal topping is lightly browned.

Preparation time 30 minutes • **Total time** 50 minutes • **Per serving** 453 calories, 7.7 g. fat (14% of calories), 2.4 g. saturated fat, 45 mg. cholesterol, 762 mg. sodium, 9 g. dietary fiber, 247 mg. calcium, 5 mg. iron, 37 mg. vitamin C, 1.8 mg. beta-carotene • **Serves 4**

TUSCAN PORK WITH WHITE BEANS

1 pound well-trimmed, lean pork
  tenderloin

¼ teaspoon freshly ground black
  pepper

⅛ teaspoon salt

1 tablespoon plus 1 teaspoon
  olive oil

½ cup sliced shallots

¼ teaspoon dried thyme or
  1 teaspoon fresh thyme

3 tablespoons balsamic vinegar

2 cans (19 ounces each)
  cannellini beans, rinsed and
  drained

1 can (14½ ounces) Italian-style
  stewed tomatoes with juice

¼ cup defatted reduced-sodium
  chicken broth

⅛ teaspoon crushed red pepper
  flakes

2 cups packed fresh spinach
  leaves or Swiss chard leaves,
  sliced

Beans have a long history in Tuscany, stretching back to the 16th century when they were first brought from the New World. White beans—cannellini—are eaten fresh when first picked in June; as the year progresses, the beans become increasingly drier, and cooking times must be adjusted accordingly. Canned beans eliminate any such guesswork from this recipe, in which the beans, bathed in a tart tomato sauce, serve as a foil for tasty pork medallions.

1 Cut the pork tenderloin crosswise into 8 pieces. Place each piece of tenderloin between 2 sheets of wax paper and pound to ½ inch thick. Sprinkle both sides of the pork with the black pepper and salt.

2 In a large no-stick skillet, warm 3 teaspoons of the oil over medium-high heat until very hot but not smoking. Add the pork and cook for 3 minutes per side, or until browned and cooked through. With a slotted spoon, transfer the pork to a plate; cover loosely to keep warm.

3 Add the remaining 1 teaspoon oil to the skillet. Add the shallots and thyme, and sauté for 1 minute. Stir in the vinegar and bring to a boil. Stir in the beans, tomatoes, broth and red pepper flakes, and return to a boil. Reduce the heat to medium-low and simmer for 5 minutes, or until slightly thickened. Stir in the spinach or Swiss chard and simmer for 1 minute, or until the spinach or chard is just wilted.

4 Divide the bean mixture among 4 plates. Top each portion with 2 pork medallions.

Preparation time 20 minutes • **Total time** 35 minutes • **Per serving** 428 calories, 10 g. fat (21% of calories), 2.1 g. saturated fat, 74 mg. cholesterol, 897 mg. sodium, 14.4 g. dietary fiber, 117 mg. calcium, 6 mg. iron, 29 mg. vitamin C, 2 mg. beta-carotene • **Serves 4**

Shallots look like miniature onions. When you remove the outer layer of skin, you'll see that they separate into cloves, like a head of garlic.

ON THE MENU
Make it a totally Tuscan meal: For starters, arrange individual salads of thinly sliced fennel and mushrooms, dressed with an olive-oil and balsamic vinaigrette. Serve whole-wheat Italian bread with the main course; and for a dessert that is quintessentially Tuscan, offer biscotti and ripe pears with a dessert wine or espresso.

KITCHEN TIP
Shallots, like garlic cloves, are easier to peel if you first blanch them in boiling water for 1 minute, then rinse them.

Main-Course Salads

❧ ❧ ❧

SOLID, SUBSTANTIAL MEALS

FEATURING PASTA AND GRAINS,

CHICKEN AND BEEF,

GREENS AND FRUIT

LAMB AND LENTIL SALAD WITH PEPPERS

1½ cups lentils, picked over and rinsed

1½ cups defatted reduced-sodium chicken broth

1½ cups water

2 garlic cloves (1 whole and 1 minced)

2 teaspoons ground cumin

½ teaspoon ground turmeric

¼ teaspoon salt

Pinch of ground cloves

¼ cup fresh orange juice

2 tablespoons fresh lemon juice

1 tablespoon plus 1 teaspoon olive oil

1 teaspoon grated lemon zest

1 teaspoon grated orange zest

½ teaspoon freshly ground black pepper

8 ounces lean, well-trimmed, boneless lamb steak, cut into 1-inch cubes

½ teaspoon dried oregano

1 jar (7 ounces) roasted red peppers, cut into julienne strips

4 scallions, thinly sliced

2 carrots, thinly sliced

2 celery stalks, thinly sliced

8 cups colorful mixed greens, torn into bite-size pieces

Thin strips of lemon zest, for garnish (optional)

There's a subtle taste of India in this rib-sticking salad: Lentils are a staple in Indian kitchens, and lamb is very popular with those who eat meat. In addition, two spices commonly found in Indian cuisine—turmeric and cumin—are used to flavor the lentils. Adding a whole garlic clove to the lentils while they cook (and then discarding it) imparts a delicate, garlicky flavor; you can use this trick any time you're cooking legumes, grains or pasta.

1 In a medium saucepan, combine the lentils, chicken broth, water, whole garlic clove, cumin, turmeric, ⅛ teaspoon of the salt and the cloves; bring to a boil over high heat. Reduce the heat to medium-low and simmer, uncovered, for 20 to 25 minutes, or until the lentils are just tender. Drain the lentils in a colander; remove the garlic clove. Return the lentils to the pan and keep warm.

2 Preheat the broiler.

3 To make the dressing, in a large bowl, whisk together the orange juice, lemon juice, oil, lemon zest, orange zest, black pepper, minced garlic and remaining ⅛ teaspoon of salt.

4 Place the lamb on the broiler-pan rack and drizzle with 1 tablespoon of the dressing. Sprinkle the lamb with the oregano. Broil the lamb 4 to 5 inches from the heat for 5 minutes, turning once, for medium-rare.

5 Meanwhile, add the peppers, scallions, carrots, celery and the reserved lentils to the bowl with the dressing and toss to mix.

6 Arrange the greens on a platter and mound the lentil mixture in the center. Spoon the broiled lamb cubes on top. Garnish with lemon zest, if desired.

Preparation time 25 minutes • **Total time** 55 minutes • **Per serving** 458 calories, 10.7 g. fat (20% of calories), 2.5 g. saturated fat, 39 mg. cholesterol, 573 mg. sodium, 11.9 g. dietary fiber, 156 mg. calcium, 11 mg. iron, 82 mg. vitamin C, 10 mg. beta-carotene • **Serves 4**

꙳ꙮ   ꙳ꙮ   ꙳ꙮ

Preceding pages: Scallop and Orange Toss (recipe on page 119).

Two-Potato Salad with Chicken

1 pound sweet potatoes, peeled and cut into 1-inch chunks

1 pound all-purpose potatoes, peeled and cut into 1-inch chunks

3 medium carrots, cut into 1-inch chunks

¼ teaspoon salt

12 ounces skinless, boneless chicken breast halves

½ teaspoon freshly ground black pepper

¼ teaspoon paprika

¼ cup reduced-calorie mayonnaise

¼ cup plain nonfat yogurt

3 tablespoons sweet pickle relish

1 tablespoon Dijon mustard

1 garlic clove, minced

1 medium green bell pepper, diced

2 celery stalks, diced

2 scallions, chopped

For an indoor-outdoor meal, grill the chicken on the backyard barbecue while the vegetables chill. You could also bring the cooked vegetables in a picnic cooler to a grilling site farther afield (at a park or beach) and prepare the dish on the spot. When time is short, you can even make the salad with grilled or barbecued chicken breast from the supermarket, or with leftover roast chicken.

1 Preheat the broiler. Spray a broiler-pan rack with no-stick spray.

2 Place the sweet potatoes, all-purpose potatoes, carrots and salt in a large saucepan with cold water to cover and bring to a boil over high heat. Reduce the heat to medium-low and simmer, covered, for 10 to 15 minutes, or until the potatoes are just tender. Drain in a colander. Spread the vegetables in a shallow baking dish and place in the freezer for 10 minutes to chill.

3 While the vegetables are chilling, sprinkle the chicken with ¼ teaspoon of the black pepper and the paprika. Place the chicken on the prepared rack and broil 4 to 5 inches from the heat, turning the pieces several times, for 6 to 8 minutes, or until cooked through. Remove from the broiler, cool briefly and cut into 1-inch pieces.

4 To make the dressing, in a large bowl, whisk together the mayonnaise, yogurt, pickle relish, mustard, garlic and the remaining ¼ teaspoon black pepper.

5 Add the chilled vegetables, bell peppers, celery and scallions to the dressing, and toss to mix. Add the chicken and toss gently.

Preparation time 35 minutes • **Total time** 45 minutes • **Per serving** 375 calories, 7.2 g. fat (17% of calories), 1.7 g. saturated fat, 57 mg. cholesterol, 468 mg. sodium, 6.7 g. dietary fiber, 91 mg. calcium, 3 mg. iron, 60 mg. vitamin C, 19.1 mg. beta-carotene • **Serves 4**

❦ ❦ ❦

ON THE MENU
You don't need to add much to this very appealing summer supper: Start with ice-cold cucumbers and onions tossed with rice vinegar, and put out bowls of chilled berries for dessert.

MEXICAN TUNA COBB SALAD

¼ cup chopped fresh cilantro

¼ cup fat-free mayonnaise

¼ cup plain nonfat yogurt

3 tablespoons drained canned chopped green chilies

2 tablespoons minced red onion

2 tablespoons fresh lime juice

1 teaspoon grated lime zest

¼ teaspoon salt

⅛ teaspoon freshly ground black pepper

8 cups Romaine lettuce, thinly sliced

1 can (19 ounces) pinto or red kidney beans, rinsed and drained

1 can (6⅛ ounces) water-packed tuna, drained and flaked

4 plum tomatoes, diced

1 small cucumber, peeled, seeded and diced

1 medium yellow or red bell pepper, diced

½ medium avocado, peeled and diced

½ cup diced radishes

2 tablespoons chopped fresh cilantro, for garnish (optional)

Baked tortilla chips (optional)

Robert Cobb, manager of the original Brown Derby restaurant, might not recognize this as the salad he invented and brought to fame back in the 1920s, but it's fun to improvise on his idea of a "chopped" salad. Here, the components are tuna, beans, tomatoes, cucumbers, bell peppers, avocado and radishes, arranged on a bed of Romaine and accented with a creamy cilantro dressing. Accompany the salad with low-fat oven-baked tortilla chips or warm corn tortillas—and be sure everyone gets a good look at this impressive salad before you dish it out.

1 To make the dressing, in a small bowl, combine the cilantro, mayonnaise, yogurt, chilies, onions, lime juice, lime zest, salt and black pepper, and whisk until blended.

2 In a large bowl, toss the lettuce with ¼ cup of the dressing.

3 Arrange the lettuce on a platter. Spoon the beans, tuna, tomatoes, cucumbers, bell peppers, avocados, radishes and some of the dressing in parallel rows on top of the lettuce. Place the remaining dressing in a small bowl to serve on the side. If desired, sprinkle the salad with chopped cilantro and serve with baked tortilla chips.

Preparation time 35 minutes • **Total time** 45 minutes • **Per serving** 231 calories, 5.2 g. fat (20% of calories), 0.8 g. saturated fat, 17 mg. cholesterol, 668 mg. sodium, 7.7 g. dietary fiber, 122 mg. calcium, 5 mg. iron, 90 mg. vitamin C, 2.7 mg. beta-carotene • **Serves 4**

❧ ❧ ❧

To seed the cucumber, first peel it, then slice it in half lengthwise.

Using the tip of a teaspoon or a melon baller, scrape out the seeds.

Sesame Noodles with Grilled Salmon

8 ounces spaghetti

6 ounces snow peas, trimmed and halved

1 tablespoon plus 2 teaspoons reduced-sodium soy sauce

1 teaspoon light brown sugar

1 teaspoon fresh lemon juice

¼ teaspoon grated fresh ginger

12 ounces skinned salmon fillet, cut into 4 equal pieces

½ cup plain nonfat yogurt

2 tablespoons reduced-fat peanut butter

2 garlic cloves, minced

½ teaspoon dark sesame oil

¼ teaspoon hot-pepper sauce

2 medium carrots, shredded

1 medium red bell pepper, cut into julienne strips

2 scallions, cut into julienne strips

½ cup loosely packed fresh cilantro leaves, chopped

Reduced-sodium soy sauce, for dipping (optional)

Cold sesame noodles—a key to the reputation of any Szechuan restaurant—make a terrific foundation for a main-dish salad. Marinated broiled salmon fillets are an unexpected and highly satisfying addition to the sauced noodles; snow peas, peppers, carrots and scallions add lots of color and crunch.

1 Preheat the broiler. Spray a broiler-pan rack with no-stick spray.

2 Bring a large covered pot of water to a boil over high heat. Add the pasta, return to a boil and cook for 8 to 9 minutes, or according to package directions until al dente. Thirty seconds before the pasta is done, stir in the snow peas. Drain the pasta and snow peas in a colander and cool briefly under gently running cold water; drain again.

3 While the pasta is cooking, combine 2 teaspoons of the soy sauce, the brown sugar, lemon juice and ginger in a shallow baking dish; add the salmon, turning to coat.

4 Arrange the salmon on the prepared broiler rack and spoon the soy mixture on top. Broil the salmon 4 to 5 inches from the heat for 8 to 10 minutes, or until lightly browned and cooked through. Remove from the broiler.

5 Meanwhile, make the dressing. In a large bowl, whisk together the yogurt, peanut butter, garlic, sesame oil, hot-pepper sauce and the remaining 1 tablespoon soy sauce until blended.

6 Add the drained pasta and snow peas, the carrots, bell peppers, scallions and cilantro to the dressing, and toss to mix. Divide the sesame noodles among 4 plates and top each portion with a piece of grilled salmon. Serve with additional soy sauce, if desired.

Preparation time 35 minutes • **Total time** 45 minutes • **Per serving** 452 calories, 10.1 g. fat (20% of calories), 1.6 g. saturated fat, 47 mg. cholesterol, 374 mg. sodium, 4.4 g. dietary fiber, 119 mg. calcium, 5 mg. iron, 67 mg. vitamin C, 6.8 mg. beta-carotene • **Serves 4**

LEMON-DILL SHRIMP CAESAR

12 slices (3½ ounces) Italian or French bread, cut ½-inch thick

3 garlic cloves (1 halved and 2 minced)

¼ cup buttermilk

3 tablespoons chopped fresh dill

1 ounce Romano cheese, coarsely grated

½ teaspoon anchovy paste

¼ teaspoon freshly ground black pepper

1 pound medium shrimp, peeled and deveined, with tails attached

2 teaspoons extra-virgin olive oil

½ teaspoon grated lemon zest

6 cups Romaine lettuce, torn into bite-size pieces

2 cups stemmed and halved cherry tomatoes

1 bunch watercress or arugula, tough stems removed

8 ounces small fresh mushrooms, sliced

Lemon slices, for garnish (optional)

Caesar salad has made a major comeback in the past few years after having been out of fashion for a decade or two: This classic salad is now turning up on restaurant menus nationwide. For an update, still-warm broiled shrimp, savory with a garlic-lemon marinade, are tossed with Romaine, watercress, cherry tomatoes and mushrooms. The dressing is a creamy dilled Caesar, minus the egg.

1 Preheat the broiler. Rub the bread slices with the halved garlic. Place the bread in a jelly-roll pan and broil 4 to 5 inches from the heat for 2 minutes per side, or until toasted. Transfer the bread from the pan to a plate, leaving the broiler on.

2 To make the dressing, in a large bowl, whisk together the buttermilk, dill, Romano, anchovy paste and black pepper; set aside.

3 Place the shrimp in the jelly-roll pan and sprinkle with the olive oil, minced garlic and lemon zest. Toss the shrimp to coat evenly and arrange in a single layer in the pan. Broil the shrimp 4 to 5 inches from the heat, turning once, for 3 to 4 minutes, or until opaque.

4 Meanwhile, add the Romaine, tomatoes, watercress or arugula and mushrooms to the bowl with the dressing and toss to mix. Add the broiled shrimp and toss gently. Divide the salad among 4 plates and serve with 3 bread slices each. Garnish with lemon slices, if desired.

Preparation time 25 minutes • **Total time** 35 minutes • **Per serving** 267 calories, 7.5 g. fat (25% of calories), 1 g. saturated fat, 148 mg. cholesterol, 441 mg. sodium, 4.6 g. dietary fiber, 257 mg. calcium, 5 mg. iron, 51 mg. vitamin C, 2.7 mg. beta-carotene • **Serves 4**

❧ ❧ ❧

FOR A CHANGE
Romaine is the usual lettuce for Cobb salad, but you could use Bibb, Boston or mesclun (a mix of colorful baby lettuce leaves) instead of the watercress or arugula called for here.

HEAD START
You can wash and dry the greens ahead of time; refrigerate them in loosely closed plastic bags. Make the dressing in advance, too, and refrigerate it in a tightly closed jar.

SMOKED CHICKEN SALAD WITH FRUIT

¼ cup fresh lime juice

1 tablespoon vegetable oil

1 teaspoon honey

⅛ teaspoon crushed red pepper flakes

¼ teaspoon grated lime zest

½ large ripe papaya, peeled and sliced (12 ounces)

2 medium plums, sliced very thin

2 plum tomatoes, sliced

2 scallions, chopped

½ teaspoon grated fresh ginger

8 cups Boston lettuce, torn into bite-size pieces

1 large bunch watercress, tough stems removed

6 ounces skinless smoked chicken breast, cut into julienne strips

2 tablespoons sliced natural almonds, toasted

The inventive partnering of plums and papaya with plum tomatoes and scallions makes this salad a standout. Savory smoked chicken and tart watercress provide a pleasing counterpoint to the sweetness of the fruit. To reduce the percentage of calories from fat, eat the salad with crusty bread. For the topping, buy almonds labeled "natural" (this means they're not blanched) and toast them in a skillet (see below).

1 To make the dressing, in a medium bowl, whisk together 3 tablespoons of the lime juice, the oil, honey, red pepper flakes and lime zest.

2 In a large bowl, combine the papaya, plums, plum tomatoes, scallions, ginger and remaining 1 tablespoon lime juice.

3 Add the lettuce and watercress to the fruit mixture, along with 3 tablespoons of the dressing, and toss to coat.

4 Add the smoked chicken to the remaining dressing and toss to coat. Divide the greens and fruit mixture among 4 plates. Top with the smoked chicken and sprinkle with the almonds.

Preparation time 20 minutes • **Total time** 20 minutes • **Per serving** 219 calories, 9.4 g. fat (36% of calories), 1.6 g. saturated fat, 38 mg. cholesterol, 451 mg. sodium, 4.6 g. dietary fiber, 184 mg. calcium, 3 mg. iron, 93 mg. vitamin C, 3.8 mg. beta-carotene • **Serves 4**

❧ ❧ ❧

To toast the almonds, place them in a small dry skillet and toast over medium heat, shaking the pan frequently.

After 5 to 10 minutes of cooking, the almonds should be golden brown and very fragrant.

Tip the almonds onto a plate so that they stop cooking, then let them cool slightly before adding them to the salad.

THAI BEEF SALAD

12 ounces lean, trimmed boneless beef sirloin or top round steak

2 garlic cloves (1 halved and 1 minced)

¼ teaspoon freshly ground black pepper

¼ cup rice wine vinegar

2 teaspoons vegetable oil

1 teaspoon dark sesame oil

1 teaspoon sugar

½ teaspoon grated fresh ginger

¼ teaspoon salt

¼ teaspoon crushed red pepper flakes

2 scallions, thinly sliced

12 cups green-leaf lettuce, torn into bite-size pieces

1 cup thinly sliced kirby or English cucumbers

1 cup loosely packed fresh cilantro leaves, chopped

1 cup loosely packed fresh mint leaves, chopped

1 small ripe mango or papaya, peeled and diced

1 cup bean sprouts

2 medium carrots, cut into julienne strips

1 tablespoon chopped unsalted dry-roasted peanuts

Lime wedges, for garnish (optional)

There is a category of delicious Thai salads called, appropriately enough, *yum:* These salads consist of greens topped with meat or poultry, fish or shellfish. *Yum gong,* for instance, comes with curry-flavored shrimp, while *yum pla muok* is made with spiced squid and pickled garlic. This dish is based on *yum nuer,* a salad topped with slices of spicy grilled beef. A sprinkling of fresh herbs is characteristic of *yums;* here, fresh cilantro and mint are added to the dressing instead.

1 Preheat the broiler. Spray the broiler-pan rack with no-stick spray.

2 Rub the steak on both sides with the halved garlic clove, then sprinkle with the black pepper. Place the steak on the prepared broiler-pan rack and broil 4 to 6 inches from the heat, turning once, for 5 minutes per side, or until medium rare. Transfer the steak to a plate and let stand for 5 minutes.

3 Meanwhile, make the dressing. In a large bowl, whisk together the vinegar, vegetable oil, sesame oil, sugar, ginger, salt, red pepper flakes and minced garlic.

4 Transfer the steak to a cutting board and pour any juices remaining on the steak plate into a medium bowl. Add 1 tablespoon of the dressing and the scallions to the juices, and stir to combine.

5 Carve the steak into ¼-inch-thick slices. Add the steak to the bowl with the scallions and toss to coat.

6 Add the lettuce, cucumbers, cilantro and mint to the dressing in the large bowl and toss to coat. Arrange the lettuce mixture on 4 plates. Mound the steak mixture on top, then top with the mangoes or papayas, bean sprouts and carrots. Sprinkle the salads with the chopped peanuts. Garnish with lime wedges, if desired.

Preparation time 25 minutes • **Total time** 30 minutes • **Per serving** 266 calories, 10 g. fat (34% of calories), 2.5 g. saturated fat, 57 mg. cholesterol, 211 mg. sodium, 4.2 g. dietary fiber, 166 mg. calcium, 6 mg. iron, 56 mg. vitamin C, 9.4 mg. beta-carotene • **Serves 4**

MIXED-GRAIN AND CHICK-PEA TABBOULEH

5¾ cups water

½ cup barley

½ teaspoon salt

½ cup instant couscous

½ cup bulgur

⅓ cup fresh orange juice

3 tablespoons red wine vinegar

1 tablespoon plus 1 teaspoon
extra-virgin olive oil

2 garlic cloves, minced

1 teaspoon honey

½ teaspoon freshly ground black
pepper

½ cup slivered dried apricots

½ cup chick-peas, rinsed and
drained

1 medium yellow bell pepper,
diced

1 cup diced kirby or English
cucumber

1 cup stemmed and halved cherry
tomatoes

4 scallions, thinly sliced

½ cup chopped Italian parsley

¼ cup chopped fresh mint

8 Boston lettuce leaves

3 ounces feta cheese, crumbled

Chopped fresh mint and mint
sprigs, for garnish (optional)

Middle Eastern *tabbouleh* is traditionally a one-grain dish, made solely from bulgur (a specially prepared form of cracked wheat), along with chopped herbs, tomatoes, lemon juice and olive oil. This "tabbouleh extraordinaire" includes other favorite Middle Eastern ingredients—couscous, barley, chick-peas and apricots, as well as a sprinkling of feta cheese. Serve the salad with wedges of pita bread or strips of seed-topped crackerbread.

1 In a medium saucepan, combine 4 cups of the water, the barley and ⅛ teaspoon of the salt, and bring to a boil over high heat. Reduce the heat to medium-low, cover and simmer for 35 minutes, or until the barley is tender. Transfer the barley to a colander, rinse under cold running water and drain.

2 While the barley is cooking, in another medium saucepan, bring the remaining 1¾ cups of water and ⅛ teaspoon of the salt to a boil over high heat. Stir in the couscous and bulgur, and remove from the heat. Cover and let stand for 10 minutes, or until the grains have absorbed the liquid. Fluff the couscous and bulgur with a fork, transfer to a jelly-roll pan and place in the freezer for 10 minutes to chill.

3 While the grains are chilling, make the dressing. In a large bowl, whisk together the orange juice, vinegar, oil, garlic, honey, black pepper and remaining ¼ teaspoon salt. Stir in the apricots.

4 Add the barley, chilled couscous and bulgur, chick-peas, bell peppers, cucumbers, tomatoes, scallions, parsley and mint to the dressing and toss well.

5 Divide the lettuce among 4 plates. Spoon the grain mixture into the center and sprinkle with the feta cheese. Sprinkle with chopped mint and garnish with mint sprigs, if desired.

Preparation time 30 minutes • **Total time** 45 minutes • **Per serving** 457 calories, 11.6 g. fat (22% of calories), 4.1 g. saturated fat, 19 mg. cholesterol, 614 mg. sodium, 13.1 g. dietary fiber, 197 mg. calcium, 5 mg. iron, 49 mg. vitamin C, 1.5 mg. beta-carotene • **Serves 4**

Scallop and Orange Toss

- 3 medium navel oranges
- 1 tablespoon plus 1 teaspoon extra-virgin olive oil
- 1 tablespoon plus 1 teaspoon red wine vinegar
- ½ teaspoon grated lemon zest
- ¼ teaspoon freshly ground black pepper
- ⅛ teaspoon salt
- 12 cups fresh spinach leaves, tough stems removed
- 4 ounces radicchio, thinly sliced
- 1 medium red bell pepper, diced
- 2 ounces trimmed Canadian bacon, finely diced
- ⅓ cup thinly sliced shallots
- 1 pound sea scallops, tough muscle removed

Eye-catching radicchio is expensive, but the firm leaves of each small head are tightly packed, so there's little waste.

Because the ingredients for this salad are few and their preparation simple, it's important that everything be of the very best quality. Take an extra moment at the market to select the plumpest scallops, the heaviest, juiciest oranges and the freshest, crispest spinach; splurge a bit on the radicchio and extra-virgin olive oil. Buy some pretty dinner rolls, too, and heat them while you make the salad. When you sit down to the meal, you'll agree it was worth every minute and the few extra pennies.

1 Using a serrated knife, pare the peel and white pith from the oranges. Working over a medium bowl, cut out the sections from between the membranes and set the sections aside. Squeeze 3 tablespoons of orange juice from the membranes into the bowl.

2 To the orange juice, add 3 teaspoons of the oil, the vinegar, lemon zest, ⅛ teaspoon of the black pepper and the salt; whisk to combine.

3 In a large bowl, combine the reserved orange sections, spinach, radicchio and bell peppers.

4 In a medium no-stick skillet, warm the remaining 1 teaspoon oil over medium-high heat. Stir in the bacon and shallots, and cook for 2 minutes, or until golden. Stir in the scallops and the remaining ⅛ teaspoon black pepper, and sauté for 2 minutes, or until the scallops are opaque. With a slotted spoon, transfer the scallop mixture to a plate.

5 Add the orange dressing to the skillet and cook, stirring, for 30 seconds to warm.

6 Add the warm dressing to the bowl with the orange sections and spinach mixture, and toss to mix. Divide the spinach mixture among 4 plates and top with the scallop mixture.

Preparation time 30 minutes • **Total time** 35 minutes • **Per serving** 268 calories, 7.3 g. fat (23% of calories), 1.2 g. saturated fat, 45 mg. cholesterol, 590 mg. sodium, 7.6 g. dietary fiber, 264 mg. calcium, 6 mg. iron, 152 mg. vitamin C, 7.8 mg. beta-carotene • **Serves 4**

PASTA, CANNELLINI AND ESCAROLE SALAD

10 ounces fusilli pasta

3 large carrots, thinly sliced

1 tablespoon plus 1 teaspoon
extra-virgin olive oil

2 ounces sliced Canadian bacon,
cut into thin strips

⅓ cup thinly sliced shallots

2 garlic cloves, minced

½ teaspoon dried thyme or
1 tablespoon fresh thyme

8 cups loosely packed cut escarole
(1-inch pieces), well washed

¼ cup defatted reduced-sodium
chicken broth

½ teaspoon freshly ground black
pepper

⅛ teaspoon salt

2 cups stemmed and halved
cherry tomatoes

1 can (19 ounces) cannellini
beans, rinsed and drained

2 tablespoons balsamic vinegar

Fresh thyme sprigs, for garnish
(optional)

Italians prize the pairing of greens and beans, as welcome in salads as it is in soups (such as minestrone) and pasta dishes. In this Italian-inspired pasta salad, robust escarole, sautéed with Canadian bacon and garlic, shares the spotlight with the large white beans called cannellini.

1 Bring a large covered pot of water to a boil over high heat. Add the pasta to the boiling water, return to a boil and cook, stirring frequently, for 9 to 11 minutes, or according to package directions until al dente. Three minutes before the pasta is done, stir in the carrots and cook until the carrots are tender. Reserving 2 tablespoons of the cooking liquid, drain the pasta and the carrots in a colander; rinse under cold running water and drain again.

2 While the pasta is cooking, in a large skillet, warm the oil over medium-high heat. Add the bacon, shallots, garlic and thyme, and sauté for 2 minutes, or until the bacon is golden. Stir in the escarole, broth, black pepper, salt and reserved pasta liquid, and bring to a boil. Reduce the heat to medium and cook, stirring, for about 1 minute, or until the escarole is tender. Transfer the escarole mixture to a salad bowl.

3 Add the drained pasta and carrots, the cherry tomatoes, beans and vinegar to the salad bowl, and toss to mix. Garnish with thyme sprigs, if desired.

Preparation time 20 minutes • **Total time** 30 minutes • **Per serving** 499 calories, 8.1 g. fat (14% of calories), 1.3 g. saturated fat, 7 mg. cholesterol, 542 mg. sodium, 13.1 g. dietary fiber, 144 mg. calcium, 6 mg. iron, 31 mg. vitamin C, 14.4 mg. beta-carotene • **Serves 4**

❧ ❧ ❧

MARKET AND PANTRY
You'll find two kinds of fusilli in the market—long and cut. Long fusilli is like curly strands of spaghetti, while cut fusilli is similar to rotelle, rotini or twists. The cut fusilli is an ideal choice for a salad such as this one.

SUBSTITUTION
You might like to use fresh spinach instead of escarole in this salad, but keep in mind that the more tender spinach leaves may cook in less than a minute. If you can't find cannellini, Great Northern beans will do.

TURKEY AND TWO-RICE SLAW

2 cups water

1 cup defatted reduced-sodium chicken broth

½ cup wild rice

1 garlic clove, crushed

1 bay leaf, preferably imported

1 cup long-grain white rice

2 tablespoons cider vinegar

1 tablespoon plus 1 teaspoon vegetable oil

1 tablespoon honey

¼ teaspoon freshly ground black pepper

⅛ teaspoon salt

2 cups shredded red cabbage

2 cups shredded green cabbage

1 cup thinly sliced fennel or celery

5 ounces skinless smoked turkey breast, diced

2 Red Delicious apples, diced

⅓ cup dried cranberries or raisins

2 scallions, thinly sliced

2 tablespoons chopped pecans

Coleslaw, that perennial picnic favorite, takes its name from the Dutch words *kool sla*, meaning cabbage salad. While both red and green cabbages are in this slaw, there's much more going on: In fact, the cabbage takes a back seat to such "exotic" ingredients as wild rice, smoked turkey, fennel and dried cranberries.

1 In a large saucepan, bring the water and broth to a boil over high heat. Stir in the wild rice, garlic and bay leaf; reduce the heat, cover and simmer for 20 minutes. After 20 minutes, stir in the white rice; cover and cook for 18 to 20 minutes longer, or until both the white and wild rice are tender.

2 While the rice is cooking, make the dressing. In a large bowl, whisk together the vinegar, oil, honey, black pepper and salt.

3 Drain the rice; remove the bay leaf and garlic. Add the rice to the bowl with the dressing and toss to mix. Stir in the red and green cabbages and the fennel or celery. Add the turkey, apples, cranberries or raisins and scallions, and toss gently. Divide the salad among 4 plates and sprinkle with the pecans.

Preparation time 25 minutes • **Total time** 40 minutes • **Per serving** 465 calories, 9.6 g. fat (19% of calories), 1.4 g. saturated fat, 18 mg. cholesterol, 720 mg. sodium, 5.8 g. dietary fiber, 83 mg. calcium, 4 mg. iron, 45 mg. vitamin C, 0.2 mg. beta-carotene • **Serves 4**

The rather heart-shaped fennel bulb is topped with stalks and feathery leaves that are usually removed before sale.

This cross-section of a fennel bulb shows its layered structure. Cut out the solid core before slicing the fennel.

ITALIAN BREAD SALAD WITH SWORDFISH

4 **cups cubed sourdough or Italian bread**

2 **garlic cloves, minced**

2 **tablespoons balsamic vinegar**

1 **tablespoon plus 1 teaspoon extra-virgin olive oil**

½ **teaspoon dried thyme**

¼ **teaspoon salt**

¼ **teaspoon crushed red pepper flakes**

12 **ounces swordfish steaks**

5 **ounces fresh spinach, tough stems removed**

1 **large bunch arugula or watercress, tough stems removed**

2 **plum tomatoes, diced**

1 **yellow or red bell pepper, sliced**

½ **medium red onion, sliced**

½ **cucumber, peeled, seeded and thinly sliced**

¼ **cup coarsely chopped fresh basil**

Bread and salad are a natural combination, but what's bread salad? It's a Tuscan dish called *panzanella*, devised as a way of using up a stale loaf. In Tuscany, dense whole-wheat bread is typically soaked in water, squeezed dry and then combined with tomatoes, herbs and dressing for a salad that's soft and soothing. This version is crisper: The fresh bread cubes are toasted like croutons.

1 Preheat the oven to 375°.

2 In a jelly-roll pan, toss the bread cubes with half the minced garlic. Bake for 10 minutes, or until golden. Remove from the oven and set aside to cool.

3 Preheat the broiler. Spray a broiler pan-rack with no-stick spray.

4 To make the dressing, in a large bowl, whisk together the vinegar, oil, thyme, salt, red pepper flakes and the remaining garlic.

5 Place the swordfish on the prepared broiler-pan rack and baste one side with 2 teaspoons of the dressing. Broil 4 to 6 inches from the heat, turning once without basting the second side, for 4 minutes per side, or until the swordfish just flakes when tested with a fork.

6 Transfer the swordfish to a cutting board and cut into 1-inch cubes.

7 Add the bread cubes, spinach, arugula or watercress, tomatoes, bell peppers, onions, cucumbers and basil to the bowl with the remaining dressing, and toss to combine. Divide the spinach mixture among 4 plates and top with the swordfish.

Preparation time 30 minutes • **Total time** 45 minutes • **Per serving** 281 calories, 9.9 g. fat (31% of calories), 1.9 g. saturated fat, 33 mg. cholesterol, 467 mg. sodium, 4.2 g. dietary fiber, 169 mg. calcium, 4 mg. iron, 79 mg. vitamin C, 3.5 mg. beta-carotene • **Serves 4**

❧ ❧ ❧

FOOD FACT
Swordfish, caught off the U.S. coasts and also in Canadian, South American and Caribbean waters, is always in good supply. Its flesh ranges from pale pink to red, but always turns ivory white when cooked.

INDEX

✄ ✄ ✄